VIETNAM
NEW PATHWAY OF AN ECONOMY

NGUYEN DINH LUONG
Copyright © 2022 Nguyen Dinh Luong

All rights reserved.

ISBN: 979-10-699-8779-1

This English book has been translated from the Vietnamese book entitled "Viet nam - Loi re cua mot nen Kinh te" -
Author: NGUYEN Dinh Luong and a group of authors -
English Translator: NGUYEN Thi Thuy Hang, English Editorial Board - Vietnamtimes - Hanoi, VIETNAM
January 28th 2022

Published on February 1st 2022 - Amazon Kindle Direct Publishing - 9.99EUR

"DEPOT LEGAL" BIBLIOTHEQUE NATIONALE DE FRANCE- JANUARY 2022

VIETNAM - NEW PATHWAY OF AN ECONOMY

CONTENTS

The most significant and difficult bilateral trade agreement has been signed by Vietnam

From the bitter past, we plant the seeds of a better future

My July 13

Three reasons for successful signing of the U.S – Vietnam BTA Agreement

The BTA and the thick shroud of smoke of war

The BTA and the missed opportunity

Light of national benefits and the "stubborn"

From burning tea cup to embarrassing negotiation for both sides

Greater challenge outside the Vietnam-U.S negotiation

The sorrow of the BTA negotiator

In my period, no one believed in Vietnam-US friendship

Story about the White House's "gift" or bittersweet memories of a photo

Three peak joys of the negotiator

Nghe An-born "plowman" in the "US-Vietnam trade field

"Match-maker" of Vietnam-US relations

Alleviating misunderstandings - building trust

PREFACE TO THE ENGLISH BOOK

Nguyen Dinh Luong was the right man for the right time in Vietnam.

Possessed of intelligence but humility and openness to learning, love of his country but understanding of the changing world, and a dedication to hard work, he was instrumental in bringing Vietnam's economy into the 21st century.

As his counterpart in negotiating the US-Vietnam BTA, I could not know this at first when we met in 1996. But as this book recounts, despite our deep differences in age, background and experience of difficult past between our two countries, we were able to come to understand each other, and to help bring our two governments and countries to understand each other better too, in a way that benefited both sides.

I have cherished and valued Luong's friendship for many years now. But what I did not fully understand until I read his book is the huge challenge he faced in preparing for our negotiations and in organizing the Vietnamese delegation to engage, and the skillful way he dealt with these challenges. I freely admit of the two of us, he had the far more difficult job in the negotiations.

I also firmly believe that without his leadership, wisdom, and vision, it could have taken many more years for Vietnam to make the transition to the modernizing developing economy that we see today.

I believe and hope that his countrymen understand and appreciate the historic role he played, and the debt they owe him.

I am glad that he has taken the time and effort to compile these recollections of that time, and I hope that future generations of Vietnamese and Americans will learn from these valuable lessons.

There is much tragedy in our past history, but I will always be grateful to Nguyen Dinh Luong for his leadership and the role we were able to play in putting that behind us.

by Joseph Damond
September 2021

1 INTRODUCTION

On July 13, 2000 in Washington, the "U.S.-Vietnam Bilateral Trade Agreement" (BTA) was signed and came into effect on December 10, 2001. The U.S.-Vietnam Trade Agreement was an critical step in order for Vietnam's process to join the World Trade Organization (WTO) and integrate into the global economy.

Compared to trade agreements that Vietnam had signed before, BTA Vietnam - U.S. agreement had a much broader scope of regulations, detailing its commitment to trade in goods, services, investment and intellectual property on the products made by citizens and legal entities from the two countries.

In 2013, former U.S. Chief Negotiator Joseph Damond published in Vietnam his book "Give Trade a Chance" in English about the five-year negotiation process. Joe Damond's 200 book pages provided readers with a perspective on the normalization of relations and cooperation and integration between Vietnam and the United States. From the positions of the "enemies without common sky", the two sides came together to search, tailor and meticulously compile each small piece of trust, hoping to create the bright and ultimately successful BTA picture as see in the book.

On the occasion of the 21st anniversary of the signing of the BTA Agreement, with the support of many friends, colleagues and the upper business community of both Vietnam and the United States, Mr. Nguyen Dinh Luong, Former Chief of the BTA negotiation team of Vietnam launched the book "Vietnam - New Pathway of an Economy". As a professional negotiator, Mr. Nguyen Dinh Luong served as The Chief of Vietnam's Negotiating Team for 5 years until the agreement was signed. About 50 of his articles and his conversations with journalists, at conferences and forums provided readers with insights into the difficult, sometimes deadlocked negotiation process which eventually succeeded.

The book is divided into 3 parts.

The first part is called ***"BTA - panoramic view of a journey"*** opening different perspectives on the U.S.-Vietnam Trade Agreement, both from the Vietnamese side and from the American perspective. Readers can see the reviews and comments of former Politburo Member, Deputy Prime Minister and Foreign Minister Nguyen Manh Cam, Former U.S. President Bill Clinton, Former U.S. BTA Chief Negotiator Joseph Damond, journalist Quang Ha, Phuong Loan, Hoang Hai Van, Huynh Phan, An Thanh... In this section, Mr. Nguyen Dinh Luong summarizes the 9 chapters and 7 appendices of this Agreement.

Part 2 ***"Still valuable lessons"*** are the conclusions of the book's author Nguyen Dinh Luong, including articles published in major Vietnamese newspapers. The articles affirm the value of the U.S.-Vietnam Trade Agreement over time by economic researchers and journalists.

Part 3 *"Economic integration viewed by negotiation expert"* is the perspective of Nguyen Dinh Luong himself. The BTA truly represents a turning point, significantly changing Vietnam's economy over the past two decades and opening the way for Vietnam to successfully integrate into the world.

The articles in the book "Vietnam - New Pathway of an Economy" will help readers fully understand why Vietnam and the United States could develop relationships that have reached the level of comprehensive partnerships as seen today. In addition, the perspective of an outsider who was directly involved in the negotiation and signing of the BTA with the United States, and over a period of 20 years of deep impacts, contemplation of what was won and lost during the effective implementation process of the agreement prompted Mr. Nguyen Dinh Luong to make up his mind to launch this book.

During the negotiations, he reached some key conclusions:

First, that the U.S. economy is strong, and the U.S. market is extremely broad and liberal, the most free one in the world. Anyone can enter the U.S. market, as long as they have goods and stay competitive. American policy is smart: open the world to competition and the American people will benefit from this.

Second, the United States dominates the world economy, dominating both the world's consumer and manufacturing trends. It's the same today.

Third, the United States dominates international organizations especially the WTO. The entire WTO legal system is transferred from the U.S. legal system. The United States, like the guardian, stands at the door of the WTO, and every single man needs to go through this door. That is also the reason why he named the book as "Vietnam - New Pathway of an Economy", as an affirmation of BTA values. Indeed, according to many leading economists, if assessed correctly, this agreement must be viewed as an important turning point for Vietnam's economy, not merely a "Turn" in his somewhat modest assessment.

The author of the book, Mr. Nguyen Dinh Luong was born in 1940 in a purely farming family in Hung Tien commune, Nam Dan district, Nghe An province. From a young age he had a reputation for being a generous and good student, and his friends at the Huynh Thuc Khang School (in Vinh) and the Moscow Institute of International Relations (MGIMO) all recognised it. After returning home from Russia, he worked as a lecturer at the Hanoi Foreign Trade University and later worked at the Ministry of Trade. With 20 years of experience in the field of international economic integration, he was personally selected by Deputy Prime Minister Tran Duc Luong to be the Chief of the BTA Negotiation Team for 5 years.

As a native of Nghe, he was well known for his frankness but during the negotiation process, he was shown to be flexible, smart, and steadfast. It was his understanding of the United States, American culture, the U.S. economy and the historical context at that time, and ultimately the goals that the U.S. negotiating team needed to achieve, along with the timely hard/soft approaches as necessary, which helped create trust among the partners themselves conclude a successful agreement.

At the beginning of the negotiation process, information and mutual understanding of each other were limited, so at some points the negotiations came to a standstill. Deputy Prime Minister Nguyen Manh Cam himself shared: "This is a massive, complex bilateral trade agreement with the greatest scope of adjustment among the trade agreements that Vietnam has signed with foreign countries". This was affirmed by Joseph Damond, former Chief Negotiator of the United States in his memoir "Give Trade a Chance", which mentioned the important role of his Vietnamese counterpart.'

Mr. Ho Tien Nghi, Former Member of the Party Central Committee, Former Assistant General Secretary, Former General Director of Vietnam News Agency commented on the book: "I find this document written very meticulously by Mr. Nguyen Dinh Luong and his team of authors, which took a lot of time and effort, and it is valuable as a library, a valuable knowledge base. Anyone who reads through this document will concur and gain much knowledge about many fields".

For that purpose, the Economic and Urban Newspaper, the speech agency of the Hanoi People's Committee sponsored the publication " Vietnam - New Pathway of an Economy".

We are pleased to introduce this book to readers and hope that the book will help us have a deeper insight into an event that is the beginning of the development and successful integration of Vietnam's economy in recent years.

Editor-in-Chief of Nguyen Minh Duc Economics and Urban Newspaper

2   PRELUDE

It was the Autumn of 1989, the season when socialist countries prepared to negotiate for the 1991-1995 five-year trade agreement. To prepare in advance, I went ahead to Moscow and met a close friend who studied with me at the Moscow Institute of International Relations (MGIMO), and who by then was the Deputy Finance Minister of the Soviet Union.

"Luong, let's talk as friends", he said. "You'd better give up the mindset of asking (for aid). You must stand tall and get rich like other people. The Soviet Union has many difficulties and is about to fall apart. There is absolutely nothing to give."

I sat still, with a bitter taste in my mouth. I took a sip of black tea that was still hot and almost burned my throat.

In the mid-80s of the last century, the Soviet Union's economic aid to Vietnam totalled about 1 billion rubles per year. "Everything will be taken care of by the Soviet Union" had become a catchphrase. No one could imagine what it would be like if aid was suddenly cut off.

In the early autumn of 2000, 11 years later, I was in the Oval Office at the White House, shaking hands with US President Bill Clinton after the Vietnam-US Bilateral Trade Agreement was signed.

What happened during those 11 years?

The Soviet Union collapsed as my friend, the Deputy Finance Minister, had warned. Aid dried up. The market of the socialist block disappeared. Due to the long-term embargo, Vietnam faced difficulties from all directions. In 1995, the turning point: the normalization of relations with the US, and then Vietnam joined ASEAN. EU countries, Japan, Korea and others started to do business with Vietnam. And in 2000, Vietnam signed a bilateral trade agreement (BTA) with the US.

The BTA negotiations, which took place between 1995 and 2000, did not only complete the "normalization" process but also opened the door for Vietnam to join the WTO and integrate into the global economy. If the declaration of the normalization of relations between the two countries in 1995 helped the US and Vietnam put behind their hostility, the BTA indeed brought the two countries together in a mutually beneficial partnership.

Signing the BTA with the US, and subsequently joining the WTO, did not only give Vietnam access to many new markets, but also accelerated drastic and far-reaching changes in our legal system, economy, and entire society. It was an emergency turnaround, one that brought Vietnam out of an historic dilemma.

The signing of the BTA was also a difficult and arduous step. A step that took nearly 5 years to complete, with dozens of rounds of negotiations, thousands of pages of text written and rewritten. It was one step, but with a full range of emotions -

from hesitation and hope to disappointment and determination to reach the destination.

One step but it was a step from hostility to partnership.

Throughout the history with consecutive wars that our nation endured, the steps we took without having to carry the sword were few.

If you consider the BTA negotiations as a long step, the "shoes" that helped Vietnam and the US overcome the difficult gap were probably the Vietnamese and American negotiators. I had the honour to be Head of Vietnam's Negotiating Team and my counterpart was Joseph Damond. A Vietnamese and an American, we were two opposites at first. We were full of doubts due to a lack of mutual understanding. The journey of negotiations had helped us to understand each other and become closer like two old friends.

In 2013, Joseph Damond published the book Give Trade a Chance. I wrote this in the introduction: Both sides aspired to sign a Bilateral Trade Agreement in order to complete the process of normalizing the US-Vietnam relationship and to build a long-term partnership and foundation for other relations.

In 2020, to reflect on the 20-year journey since the signing of the BTA, I have completed a book entitled Vietnam - New Pathway of an Economy.

The book — comprising my writings and writings by the former US Chief Negotiator Joseph Damond, comments from Former US President Bill Clinton and Former Deputy Prime

Minister Nguyen Manh Cam, interviews with me, Mr. Damond and others — recounts the difficult and lengthy negotiations, the troubles of a Vietnam that was transforming its economy, the doubts from the two former enemies who held many grudges, the clever tricks and tactics of the negotiators who ended up "walking the wire" for five years, and all the disappointing moments right through to the very end that was happy just like a dream.

This book contains macro assessments about the new generation of free trade agreements and the trend of economic integration in the new context, as well as many interesting, seemingly small behind-the-scene details that nevertheless could have influenced the course of history.

Whilst curating contents for this book, I noted some repetitions in various articles published in different newspapers. These might annoy readers, but they have not been edited out due to respect for the authors and for the integrity of the articles. Hopefully, the readers can overlook this small annoyance.

I hope this small book will help those interested to better understand the BTA and Vietnam's international economic integration, and also understand how a historic step has brought together the two former enemies to become partners in the most fundamental area of all relations: trade.

Hanoi, November 2020
Nguyen Dinh Luong

PART 1

VIETNAM - U.S. BILATERAL TRADE AGREEMENT - PANORAMIC VIEW OF THE JOURNEY

The most significant and difficult bilateral trade agreement has been signed by Vietnam

Nguyen Manh Cam - *Former Deputy of Politburo, former Deputy Prime Minister cum Minister of Foreign Affair, who led the negotiation on the BTA.*

One year since Vietnam and U.S's diplomatic relation normalization, the two countries had conducted the negotiation of a trade agreement to fully finish the process of normalization between them.

After the 5-year negotiating, on July 13, 2000, the Agreement was signed and took effect at the end of 2001 when approved by the two countries' Congresses.

The BTA is considered to be the most voluminous, complicated with the largest scope of regulations among those have been signed by Vietnam with other countries.

It is a legal corridor to operate the economic - trade relations between Vietnam and the United States - the biggest and most modern economy in the world.

The BTA creates opportunities for U.S businesses to access the Vietnamese market and vice versa for Vietnamese businesses entering a giant market of import – export, investment and accessing the modern science and technology.

When accessing the US economy, Vietnamese businesses are motivated to innovate their technology and management, improve productivity, products' quality and prestige in the market.

Not only does the BTA help renew Vietnam's legal regime of economic regulating for its development, promoting the strengthening of multiple relations between Vietnam and the US, but it also has had a strong effects on the foreign trade relations of Vietnam and others in the world.

The Vietnam – U.S trade agreement is one key step for Vietnam to join the World Trade Organization (WTO) and stimulate Vietnam's economic development to integrate into the global economic arena.

From the bitter past, we plant the seeds of a better future

"The Agreement is the one reminding that the former foes can possibly reconcile and together seek for common interests to their people, leave the past behind and embrace the future, forgiving and reconciliation"

The speech made by US President Bill Clinton at the press-release after the Vietnam – U.S. BTA was signed - CNN broadcast 13th July 2001

Good afternoon, ladies and gentlemen! Just a few moments ago, Ambassador Barshefsky and Minister Vu Khoan signed the agreement between the United States and Vietnam, that will dramatically open Vietnam's economy for the integrated international community and create trade between our two nations. And so, from the bitter past, we plant the seeds of a better future.

This is another historic step in the process of normalization, reconciliation and healing between our two nations. Improvement of the relationship between the United States and Vietnam has depended, from the beginning, on the progress of determining the fate of Americans that did not return from the war.

In 1994, with the support of members of Congress standing with me here and others, I lifted the trade embargo on Vietnam as the response to cooperation on the POW/MIA issue. A year later, I normalized the diplomatic relations between the two nations to further this goal. For the progress later in 1996, I appointed the former congressman Peterson – himself from former prisoner of war – to be the United States Ambassador in Vietnam.

With the indispensable help of key Congressional allies especially Senator John Kerry, Senator John McCain, Senator Bob Kerry, Senator Chuck Hagel, Senator Chuck Robb, Representative Rich Boucher, Representative Reyes (presents here), Representative Manzullo, Representative Lane Evans Colby, Bereuter and McDermott, this process has worked.

Since 1993, we have already undertaken 39 joint recovery appreciations in Vietnam, and the number of 40 is on the way as we speak. 135 American families have received the remains of their loved ones, and in the process we have found 150 parts of such remains. Time and again, the Vietnamese people have shared their memories with Americans. And we, too, have helped Vietnam in the search for answers.

Our nation also feels a special sense for responsibility to those people in Vietnam whose families were torn apart during and after the war. In the last few years, we made tremendous progress in resettling ten thousands of refugees in the United States and closing another painful chapter.

And Vietnam has done much to turn its face to the changing world. It is working to open the economy to move in the mainstream of Southeast Asia as the member of ASEAN and APEC. Our trading relations have also grown . When I took up office, export to Vietnam was only total $ 4 million, today it has extended to $ 291 million.

The agreement we signed today will dramatically open Vietnam's market on everything, from agriculture to industrial goods, telecommunication products, and creating jobs in both Vietnam and the United States.

With this agreement, Vietnam agrees to speed its opening to the world, subject to the important decisions on the rules of law in the international trade system, to increase the flow of information to its people, by inviting competition, and to accelerate the rush of free market economy and private sector in Vietnam itself. We hope the expanded trade will go hand in hand with strength and respect of human right of labour standards. As we are living in an age of well-generated but free exchange ideas, stability depends on democratic choices. By signing the agreement, Vietnam takes an important step in the right direction.

We have been working on the agreement since 1996, and many people deserve recognition. I want to say special thanks to our trade representatives, Ambassador Barshefky deputy representative of USTR Richard Fisher, Joseph Damond of USTR for working so hard in the last 4 years to turn the agreement into reality.

I would also like to thank the Vietnamese counterparts: Trade Minister Vu Khoan, Chief Negotiator Nguyen Dinh Luong. And I want to say special words of thanks also to the Vietnamese Ambassador Le Van Bang and to our Ambassador Pete Peterson, who have worked so hard to build ties of our two nations and peoples.

And, let me say again, it is my opinion that none of this would have been possible if it had not been for the visionary, brave and reconciling leadership of the Americans and the United States Congress who served, and many of whom suffering in Vietnam, especially those here with me and the other names I mentioned earlier. Our debt to them as a nation is immense.

This agreement is one more reminder that the former adversaries can come together to find common ground in a way that benefits the people, to let go over the past and embrace the future, to forgive and to reconcile. As all of you know, these days we have tried to achieve at Camp David on what many believe the most difficult to solve in all circumstances.

This day is encouraging to me, and I will take the energy after here to all of these people back to Camp David and make the argument they should follow it.

Thank you very much!

(President B.Clinton wanted to mention the meeting of leaders of Palestine and Israel occurring that time in Camp David organized by the US President – ND)

Overall picture of negotiation for Vietnam – U.S. BTA

Nguyen Dinh Luong

Part I: The context

1. The United Stated is a specific partner

At the time, the Vietnamese people had very different views and evaluations of the United States, from various perspectives on war, history, philosophy, and economics. ..etc.

I learned about the United States from the country's famous Declaration of Independence in 1776. The Declaration is so globally impactful that it was quoted by President Ho Chi Minh in the Declaration of Independence giving birth to the Democratic Republic of Vietnam. - the nation of a heroic people with a glorious 4,000year history, bravely and courageously fighting foreign invaders for independence, but in the depths of slavery without a name on the world map.

The Declaration says: All men are created equal, they are endowed by their Creator with certain inalienable Rights, among these are Life, Liberty and the pursuit of Happiness.

The Liberty and Equality are endowed by the Creator, the rights endowed by the Creator equally, neither civilians getting less nor kings getting more, the Creator endows me a right, I have that right, and no one is able to dispossess me of it.

The United States is supposed to be a "younger" nation than Vietnam. The United States was just born on July 4, 1776, in September 1786 it had constitution and in March 1789 its first national election was held. In September 1789, the first US Congress enacted the world's first Bill of Rights including: freedom of speech, freedom of press, protection of private assets.

The United States' entire legal system of civil and criminal matters is designed and built to fully grasp the spirit of the Declaration of Independence. That is freedom, equality.

* On politics and society

Both the American society and ideology are imbued with freedom: Those who are inclined to do politics should strive to be the president, to become an official, regardless of skin color or race. Those who are inclined to do business strive to become millionaires and billionaires. Whoever has scientific capacity strives to be a scientist.

All are equal, and the society recognizes a person through his/her human dignity leaving for human beings.

People are free to speak out what they love or hate, freely express their thinking despite criticizing their Presidents.

The United States has its own methods and quantifying means for the community and society's ideology, thought, also that is American power. Any ideology, desire, or wants having large majority in the society are considered by American representatives, which are its governance operation's guidelines.

However, the public opinion was sometimes deceived as the case of Vietnam war, American people were deluded by 5 Presidents to get deeply involved in the war.

*** On economy**

The American Dream of getting rich with the country's diversified resources, the legal system protecting free and equal competition are the factors creating the U.S. economy as the most powerful one in the world.

On Agriculture: Only by 2% of population with 1% of which doing business in farming directly, does the United States possess the biggest and most modern agriculture in the world, dominating the global market of corn, soybeans, wheat and cotton.

On Industry: The United States' manufacturing industry is the strongest in the world, and its digital technological industry leads the world.

The Dow Jones, Nasdaq and dollar values are still determining the pulse and frequency of the world economy. Despite increasingly fierce competition, the US economy is still the number one with a strong influence on the global economy and determines the rules of the game in many bilateral and multilateral economic relations.

Therefore, the United States is such a specifically unique partner that Vietnam has never seen another one like it.

2. Vietnam – US relationship is a specific one

It can be said that there is not any international political relationship as special as the one of the two countries Vietnam – US. The special difference is due to the serious consequences of war and suffering on both sides.

On the Vietnam side:

The country has never faced such a destructive, cruel war causing a such a large number of tragic results as the Vietnam War made by the United States. There is no family that did not lose a member's life. Millions of people died from lethal weapons. Martyr monuments are seen everywhere throughout the country.

The nation is haunted deeply in its heart with the paint of war though nearly half of century has passed away since the war's end.

On the U.S. side:

The U.S. history includes many wars but never being loser. In the Vietnam War, it was the first time the United States lost, and lost to a country with an economy, defense considered the poorest; it was also lost at the time the United States was supposed to be the world' most powerful in defense, economy, and proud of its winning tradition.

The Vietnam War smashed the golden battlefield "American Values" - the endless pride of Americans.

The Vietnam War monument in central Washington park, built with donations from American veterans in memory of more than 58,000 soldiers who died or went missing in a distant battlefield, must have not been a monument of victory.

That was an unhealable blow to the United States.

On that basis, the restoring of economic relations between two countries was not easy.

3. Considering the overall context, Vietnam needed an economic exit, and the US played an extremely important role.

During the last century's 70s – 80s, the capitalist world - economy very rapidly developed, producing "economic miracles" like Japan, which caused a stir in the US in the late 1980s, forcing the US to quickly switch to a soft economy to maintain its dominant role in the world economy.

Following the Asean economic dragons, tigers appeared such as South Korea, Taiwan, Singapore, Hong Kong and especially China.

Western Europe's economy developed strongly in the framework of an EU single market, and the single European currency Euro was introduced.

During that period, the socialist sector still maintained and was consistent with socialist economic path, the economy of State – monopoly, central planning, State – subsidizing and generally operating in the entire system with the formation of the COMECON bloc (SEV).

Due to the lack of competition and no productivity growth, the production level, it was difficult to improve product quality, causing more obstacles for raising living standards.

Socialism did not win against Capitalism in labor productivity, plus for many subjective and objective reasons led to the collapse of socialism in the late 90s.

Vietnam was an economy with its back to the wall due to its ineffective policies and decades of continuous embargo.

When socialism collapsed in Soviet and Eastern Europe, Vietnam was facing more and more difficulties.

Based on the awareness of:" The market economy is not the capitalist economy's product but the result of human society", our Party advocated the policy to develop the Vietnamese economy in the direction of the socialist-oriented market economy and has gained some achievements. However, it has to continue researching and deciphering to correctly define what the socialist-oriented market economy is.

Our Party advocated integrating into the world economy, taking part in the economic globalization, and promoting the Vietnam's economy to connect with the global economy for development.

That was a revolution. Revolution always faces obstacles.

After the Cold War ended, the world saw a race between countries to develop, competing to open their economies for integration. Globalization unfolded as a climax. The World Trade Organization (WTO) was born. Countries that had not been members yet rushed for negotiations to join the WTO.

Also at that time, the United States was dominating the world economy; controlling the world economic organizations, managing and controlling the WTO, and no countries could join the WTO without the US's consent.

Furthermore, Vietnam's integration would be really significant and realize great benefits if the country could access the American market. Only by opening up the US market, could Vietnam step up to open the EU and the world markets. If the US market did not open for Vietnam, it meant the WTO would still close its doors to Vietnam. Integration could not be considered without joining the WTO.

Part II: NEGOTIATION AND IMPLEMENTATION OF THE AGREEMENT

I. Negotiating the Vietnam – US Trade Agreement in the world dominated by the United States

Since the beginning of the BTA negotiation, the US made one has asked for a clear request: The BTA must ensure the principle of "win -win" or mutual benefit.

Vietnam was requested to have a the market economy following the WTO's standards for US businesses to enter and have full access to the country's market. The United States would open its market for Vietnam according to the WTO standards, and Vietnam would do so gradually, vice versa.

The WTO standards or WTO principles include:

- MFN - Most Favored Nation.

- NT - National treatment.

- Fair competition.

- Open the economy, open the market.

These principles are contained in the GATT-47 (The General Agreement on Tariffs and Trade signed in 1947 in La Habana – Cuba). The GATT-47 became the only institution governing the multilateral trading system and has undergone a process of development, through 8 rounds of negotiations that expanded to GATT-94. The GATT-94's operating principles became the basic principles in the World Trade Organization (WTO - born on January 1, 1995). In addition to the

GATT-94, the WTO has additional areas of agreement, including the fields of intellectual property, textiles, agriculture, etc.

It had totally 13 Agreements and 5 Annexes

In the international arena, powerful trading countries impose rules of games as a matter of course.

The GATT-47 was formed after World War II when the US economy accounted for 52% of the capitalist world economy, 47% of the world economy, the US dollar became the free world's currency with the exchanged value of the dollar to gold at $35 an ounce; the American program called the Marshall Plan providing aids for the Western and Japan to rebuild their economy after the war.

The American powers of economy, military, and politic were enough to set the rules of the game worldwide.

Meanwhile, the American legal system was stable. The US had already had a complete legal framework regulating the market economy.

In 1890, the US passed the Sherman Antitrust Act then amended by the Clayton Antitrust Act in 1914, with the Federal Trade Commission Act of 1914 signed into law to form a complete system of competition law outlawing unfair methods of competition and unfair acts or practices that affect commerce.

In 1916, the US had the "Antidumping Act of 1916".

In 1930 the United States had the Countervailing Duty (CVD).

These were also the main rules of law in the GATT-47 and then developed into WTO rules. The rules of law's approach and content of the GATT- 47 and the WTO did not impact on the US legal framework, as it was developed from the US law. In other words, the United States has internationalized American rules into the world rules.

II. The Agreement – a must for attention

The BTA contains 7 Chapters, 9 Annexes, 1 exchanged letter.

Inside, there are 4 most basic Chapters:

1. Trade in goods

2. Trade in services

3. Protection of intellectual property rights

4. Development of investment relationships

* Attentions should be paid in the Agreement

1. Though the BTA was signed according to the WTO rules, there is not the Agreement of Investment in the WTO rules, which the BTA contains. The WTO has only the Agreement on Trade-Related Investment Measures (TRIMs) – some aspects relating investment. The WTO is a trade organization, and is handed over the authority to deal with investment issues by member countries.

- So, why does the BTA contain the chapter of investment relationship development? On the US side, that must be the way to "circumvent establisch rights under the law". In the Unites States, the investment agreement negotiations with foreign countries must be guided by the Congress, not assigned by the Government.

At that time, the United States had the "Fast Track" Amendment, Congress empowered the Government to negotiate trade agreements with foreign countries within the law framework, Congress only ratified or not ratified.

If the chapter Development of Investment Relations is included in the BTA, without exceeding the permitted U.S. legal regulations, it will be submitted to the Congress for approval.

- Besides, both the US and Vietnam wanted the content of investment in the BTA.

2. The BTA's Intellectual Property Right (IPR) is not the IPR's entire content. The broader set of IPR rules were later addressed according to the TRIPS agreement – economically trade aspects of the IPR in the WTO.

In order to protect and enforce all aspects of IPR, signatories must fully accede to international conventions of IPR (Geneva Phonograms Convention, Berne Convention for the Protection of Literary and Artistic Works, Paris Convention on Industrial Property, UPOV Convention for the Protection of Varieties and Plants,   Convention Relating to the Distribution of Program-Carrying Signals Transmitted by Satellite, etc.) .

3. All of these chapters apply the Most Favored Nation MFN and National Treatment NT principles. The United States

alone did not commit to MFN treatment in the Intellectual Property chapter. The United States did discriminate against different countries in high-end scientific equipment (that is, exports of certain high-technology equipment are limited by the United States to certain countries for national security reasons).

4. The National Treatment – "NT" principle was an absolutely new concept in Vietnam.

In Vietnam's dictionaries (including popular or specialized ones), there was no such a concept. In magazines of that time, the term was translated differently as "national people treatment", "nation treatment", "citizen treatment".

- The principle of National Treatment requires equal treatment of locals and foreigners. The NT requests the state to commit foreign countries to be able to make use of Vietnam's legal system for their rights to be surely enforced. Also, WTO has the Trade Policy Review Body. That violates Vietnam's principles of independence and legal autonomy, and is opposed to Vietnam's policy of economic autonomy.

- Colliding with Vietnam's entirely current legal system.

By accepting this principle, did Vietnam have to dismantle the country's legislative framework and rearrange and renew everything.

III. The Agreement – Basic contents

1. Chapter of Trade in Goods

Vietnam agrees to step by step open its market, practice freedom, equality, and non-discrimination in trade.

This provision was unlike the law on commerce that Vietnam already had and differentiated from commitments in trade agreements that Vietnam had previously signed with other countries.

Regarding to the "Most Favored Nation" treatment, the Agreement reads:

"Each Party shall accord immediately and unconditionally to products originating in or exported to the territory of the other Party treatment no less favorable than that accorded to like products originating in or exported to the territory of any third country in all matters relating to:

- Customs duties and charges of any kind imposed on or in connection with importation or exportation, including the method of levying such duties and charges;

- Methods of payment for imports and exports, and the international transfer of such payments;

- Rules and formalities in connection with importation and exportation, including those relating to customs clearance, transit, warehouses, and transshipment;

- Taxes and other internal charges of any kind applied directly or indirectly to imported products;

- Laws, regulations, and other requirements affecting the sale, offering for sale, purchase, transportation, distribution, storage, and use of products in the domestic market;

- The application of quantitative restrictions and the granting of licenses."

The Most Favored Nation treatment does not apply to:

- Advantages accorded by free trade areas that a Party is a member of.

- Advantages accorded for frontier traffic.

On National Treatment:

In order to accord goods from the other Party meaningful competitive opportunities with respect to domestic competitors, each Party shall administer tariff and non-tariff measures, and shall not:

- Impose internal taxes and charges on the products of the other Party in excess of those applied to like domestic products.

- Treat products originating in the territory of the other Party less favorable than domestic products in all respects: laws, regulations, and other requirements affecting their internal sale, offering for sale, purchase, transportation, distribution, domestic storage, or use.

Vietnam commited to a schedule to reduce tariff and non-tariff barriers, create conditions for domestic and U.S. enterprises to have more freedom in import and export.

2. Chapter on Intellectual Property Rights

Those who played key roles in this Chapter's success are: Pham Dinh Chuong, former Director of the National Office of Intellectual Property of Vietnam - Ministry of Science and Technology, Do Khac Chien, Deputy Director of the Copyright Office - Ministry of Culture, Sports and Tourism, and their staffs.

- The biggest difficulty was the opposition from different sectors that capitalist countries had so far freely used and utilized inventions and creations of others to develop, yet then they used the TRIPS agreement to "handcuff" the poor including us, which was unfair and not "fair play".

- The need for Vietnam to protect and enforce fully and strictly provisions in this chapter found burdensome due to the country's improper administration of intellectual property products.

About National Treatment, the Agreement states:

- Each Party shall accord to nationals of the other Party treatment no less favorable than it accords to its own nationals with regard to the acquisition, protection, enjoyment, and enforcement of all intellectual property rights and any benefits derived therefrom.

- The Agreement comprehensively states each Party's responsibilities that need to be implemented to protect the full enforcement of intellectual property rights and related rights:

- Copyright and Related Rights

- Trademarks

- Patents

- Layout Designs (Topographies) of Integrated Circuits

- Confidential Information (Trade Secrets)

- Industrial Designs

- Vietnam agrees to soon complete procedures to fully join international conventions on intellectual property that the country has not yet been a member of.

3. Chapter on Development of Investment Relations

Those who contributed to this chapter's success are: Dr. Dinh Van An, Director General of Department of Investment Law– Ministry of Planning and Investment (MPI), who is currently assistant to the General Secretary; Tran Hao Hung, current Director General of the Department of International Cooperation– MPI and some specialists of the Department of Investment Law, MPI.

- The chapter of Development of Investment Relations in the BTA differs from the 19 investment protection agreements Vietnam had signed with other nations up to that time, including developed countries.

- It also differs from regulations already stated in Vietnam's law on investment at that time.

- As proposed by the US, both sides agreed to take the Model Investment Treaty that the United States signed in NAFTA (North American Free Trade Agreement, which includes the US, Canada, Mexico), excerpts key provisions, and design a schedule suitable for Vietnam.

- Definitions put in the chapter were completely new to Vietnam, yet suitable with international and modern norms.

For example:

"Investment" definition

Investment did not only mean contributing money to joint ventures as stated in Vietnam's Law on Investment at that time.

Investment consists of:

- A company or enterprise

- Shares, stock, and other forms of equity participation, and bonds, debentures, and other forms of debt interests, in a company

- Contractual rights, such as under turnkey, construction or management contracts, production or revenue sharing contracts, concessions, or other similar contracts

- Tangible property, including real property, and intangible property, including rights, such as leases, mortgages, liens, and pledges

- Intellectual property, including copyrights and related rights, trademarks, patents, layout designs (topographies) of integrated circuits, encrypted program-carrying satellite signals, confidential information (trade secrets), industrial designs and rights in plant varieties; and

- Rights conferred pursuant to law, such as licenses and permits

"Company" definition

Unlike in Vietnam's law, "company" is defined as "any entity constituted or organized under applicable law, whether or not for profit, and whether privately or governmentally owned or controlled, and includes a corporation, trust, partnership, sole proprietorship, branch, joint venture, association, or other organizations".

Regulations on National Treatment and Most-Favored Nation Treatment

"With respect to the establishment, acquisition, expansion, management, conduct, operation and sale or other disposition of covered investments, each Party shall accord treatment no less favorable than that it accords, in like situations, to investments in its territory of its own nationals or companies (hereinafter "national treatment") or to investments in its territory of nationals or companies of a third country (hereinafter "most-favored nation treatment"), whichever is most favorable (hereinafter "national and most favored nation treatment").

Vietnam's investment at that time had not yet recognized "National treatment". Besides, "each Party shall at all times accord to covered investments fair and equitable treatment and full protection and security, and shall in no case accord treatment less favorable than that required by applicable rules of customary international law."

About dispute settlement

"Each Party shall provide companies and nationals of the other Party with an effective means of asserting claims and enforcing rights with respect to covered investments."

The agreement also clearly states steps to assert claims and agencies competent in settling disputes, which includes international arbitrations.

About expropriations and compensation for war damages

The agreement clearly states when a country can expropriate. It points out that expropriations come with compensation, how to compensate an expropriation, and at what price.

Vietnam commits to following a schedule to eliminate all ongoing regulations that discriminate, impede freedom and fair competition in investment, such as:

- Only joint ventures are allowed to establish, no company of 100% foreign investment is licensed.

- Investment must attach to domestic materials.

- Investment products must be exported or partly exported.

- Only powerful foreign currencies are allowed to be used in investment

- Joint-stock companies are not allowed to establish, company must not issue shares or bonds.

- Either the general director or deputy general director must be Vietnamese.

- Vietnam also agrees to immediately eliminate discriminatory prices and fees such as electricity, water, air transport, port, registration of motor vehicles, tourist services, telecommunications, installation of telephones.

- In general, to comply with commitments in the Development of Investment Relations chapter, Vietnam had to rewrite its Law on Investment with a new and modern approach.

4. Chapter on Trade in services

Lawyer Nguyen Hong Duong – Ministry of Commerce took credits for this chapter. Duong was in charge of reconstructing the chapter, making it more suitable with Vietnam's conditions based on service information provided by the professional experts.

- The chapter's contents and terms were completely new to Vietnam.

- While service industries were developing speedily and strongly, even accounting for 50-70% in some countries' GDP, services in Vietnam didn't ring any bells. In Vietnam, services such as banking, transportation were still considered as links between manufacturing and consumption but no services had been regulated and managed under an official law.

- The U.S side gave us a draft with many new definitions, taking us plenty of time to study.

- The U.S draft was designed based on a high standards that had already applied in NAFTA. That means all service sectors enjoyed openness and freedom, of which Vietnam needed to make a reservation, in any area, must make a list for join negotiation.

We couldn't make the "reservation list" unless Vietnam had regulations or law for such services.

After months of carefully studying the WTO and agreements of similar countries in the WTO, we rewrote and designed a new Chapter of Trade in Services in a way that doing whatever we could, and Vietnam only made commitments step by step according to a feasible schedule.

When receiving the draft of Vietnam's delegation, the U.S side got surprised due to possibly unprecedented case of negotiation they had faced. They had to hold a seminar with consulting experts. After the seminar, the Vietnam's draft was recognized correct, allowing it to be accepted for bilateral negotiation.

Vietnam committed to open 9 service fields following a roadmap of step-by-step gradually opening according to its own strength.

5. *Relating to international disputes in investment and trade*

In the negotiation, our delegation was supported by the Ministry of Justice's experts, among them, lawyer Nguyen Khanh Ngoc, working as the Director of Department of International Cooperation at that time and currently is Ministry of Justice's Acting Deputy Minister, made the most significant contribution.

IV. Vietnam implemented the agreement

After the agreement was signed, Vietnam's National Assembly ratified and issued resolution "NQ48/2001-QH10 on amending and supplementing legal documents according to the schedule of Bilateral Trade Agreement between Vietnam and The United States".

Accordingly, the Government assigned the Ministry of Justice to host and coordinate with ministries and agencies to review and compare all legal documents with provisions in the agreement before submitting the law-making program to the National Assembly.

The National Assembly's 2001 – 2005 tenure had to newly built, supplement and amend laws, ordinances, resolutions in all fields of economy, society, science and technology, criminal, civil affairs, and administration.

According to the aforementioned resolution, the National Assembly carried out a new law-making program with a new spirit and approach, which are:

1. Vietnam supplemented and amended its almost its entire legal system, of which, basic laws such as the Civil Code, Criminal Code, Law on Intellectual Property, Law on Investment, Law on Commerce…were prioritized in a modern approach.

I would like to draw your attention to some examples:

The first basic principle in the 1995 Civil Code is "Respect for the State and public benefits,.." while respecting personal interest follows long after. In contrast, , the 2005 Civil Code (amended based on BTA direction) confirms from its first lines that: The first basic principle is "Principles of free and voluntary undertaking and agreement…are equally guaranteed by law", followed by regulations which state that "Individual right to freedom of business shall be respected and protected by law. Individuals shall have the right to choose the forms, areas, and lines of business, to establish enterprises, to freely enter into contracts and hire employees, and other rights in accordance with the provisions of law" (The Civil Code) and then "Principle of trader" equality before the law in commercial activities" (Law on Commerce) and "Investors shall be permitted to invest in all sectors and in all industries and trades which are not prohibited by law" (Law on Investment).

Since then, Vietnam laws have been designed based on principles of respecting a citizen's freedom, which is the core of a modern market economy. That is also the "American colors" found unavailable before.

Also, Vietnam has significantly reduced metaphysical, theoretical, and vague regulations in its law system and replaced them with clear, intelligible, adaptable, applicable one for a market economy. The National Assembly can only "press the button" to pass a draft after it is commented on by relevant citizens and enterprises.

2. Vietnam has transfered service activities in the economy into service industries for doing business and development.

Before signing the BTA, services such as banking, insurance, transport, postal, telecommunication were only service activities supporting production and consumption without a separate law regulating them.

After the BTA was signed, based on a new awareness of the service industries' role in the economic development process, and according to commitments stated in the BTA, Vietnam had to open service industries and built specialized laws to regulate their operations.

A series of new specializations were born, creating a legal corridor for citizens to freely do business, including the Law on Credit Institutions, Law on Securities, Law on Insurance Business, Laws on airways, maritime, etc. Service businesses have quickly developed and are playing an increasingly important role in the Vietnamese economy, especially in telecommunications, finance services, tourism, trucking, air transport..etc..

Final sprints of the negotiation marathon

"The two Ministers shook hands, and four and a half years of negotiation effectively came to an end the morning of July 10, 2000, one day short of exactly five years since diplomatic relations were restored. Luong and I exchanged broad smiles.". Joseph Damond

Joseph Damond is the Chief negotiator of the U.S. BTA negotiation delegation. After a long process of negotiating, Joseph Damond and Nguyen Dinh Luong, the Chief Negotiator of the Vietnamese BTA negotiation delegation, have become special close friends.

The article below is cited from a book named "Give Trade a Chance", written by Joseph Damond about the last stage of the negotiation. It reveals last-minute intense details of the process to sign the greatest bilateral trade agreement between Vietnam and the United States since the end of the war.

Heading to July

While I felt fairly sure that Vu Khoan would respond positively to Charlene's letter – we were hearing that he was prepared to come to Washington, our embassy in Hanoi again tried to complicate matters. A cable was dispatched arguing that Vietnam's intention were still unclear, and recommending that preconditions be attached to any visit by Minister Vu Khoan to Washington. I viewed this as being unhelpful. The embassy was proposing a negotiation before the negotiation, and Vietnam, regardless of its intentions, was sure to reach negatively. Vu Khoan had been commissioned to bring the agreement home, I reckoned, but he would have trouble getting Leadership consensus on an explicit set of preconditions before he even departed. For one thing, there was still some uncertainty about Washington's desire to sign. Charlene and Richard agreed with this analysis, seeing it as just so much amateurish interference by the embassy (other agencies in Washington agreed), and so no preconditions were sent.

Before too long, we heard back from Hanoi that Vu Khoan was indeed prepared to come to Washington.

After some back and forth, it was decided that Luong and his team would arrive on July 3 (naturally, spoiling our holiday week), and the Minister a day later. I would meet first with Luong, to scope out the situation, and Charlene and Vu Khoan would have their first meeting on July 6.

The Final Stretch: July 3-13

Luong arrived with a fairly large team of negotiators, representing all key agencies. My job of course in meeting him was to remind him and his team that our deal last July was final, with the possible exception of the three areas in which Ambassador Barshefsky had indicated in her May 17 letter that we might have flexibility.

Thus, when the full teams met on July 3, I pretty much knew what to expect, and so did Luong. Luong began the formal presentation by thanking us for our "positive response" which allowed this meeting to take place, and to say that he did not consider this meeting a "renegotiation". In fact, Luong said that it was perfectly natural that the two sides meet to discuss finalization of the agreement in principle reached last year. He then noted that the decision to send his Minister to Washington was not an easy one, "If he goes home without a deal, it will have an adverse effect on our relationship."

Luong began by discussing four broad policy concerns, and asking for our consideration. First, he repeated the concern that in exchange for all of the commitments Vietnam was undertaking, it was only receiving an annually renewable "normal trade relations" (NTR) treatment. In turn, Vietnam was granting the United States "permanent" NTR status for tariffs. Secondly, Luong noted that the United States had taken no position on whether it would grant Vietnam access to its preferential tariffs scheme for developing countries (i.e., tariffs treatment better than that received by developed country partners – an exception to NTR called our Generalized System of Preferences, or GSP program). Third, Luong raised the issue of textiles. The United States had taken an exception from MFN treatment in the agreement in this area, that allowed it to apply import quotas on textiles from Vietnam in the future, as it did to just about every other textile producer in the world. Luong repeated a request that this exception be deleted from the agreement.

Finally, Luong raised concerns about Vietnam's accession to the WTO.

Significantly, he began by talking about telecommunications services, saying that Vietnam would now like to limit U.S. participation to a maximum of 49% in this sector. I knew that the telecommunications commitments were legitimately a serious political concern within Vietnam. The fact that China had not agreed to allow U.S. majority ownership in some key telecom sectors in its WTO negotiation. In short, Vietnam had gone beyond what its larger and more developed neighbor the north had agreed to in the WTO – and this was simply politically unacceptable.

On the issue of Vietnam's eligibility for trade preferences under the "GSP" program, our hands were tied legally. The law governing this program (which I had ministered a few years before, incidentally) stated that communist developing countries could only be even considered for GSP eligibility after their accession to the WTO (no such requirement for other developing countries). All we promise Vietnam is that we would consider its eligibility in accordance with our existing law.

….After the respite of the July 4 holiday, I met Luong again on the morning of July 5, to access the situation, and begin to prepare for the meeting of our two Ministers. Luong began by telling me that he had informed his Minister that we had set an "open, frank atmosphere" in our talks, and that Vu Khoan was quite pleased to hear that we were engaged and interested in making progress. This was quite positive news, I thought, given how little substantive satisfaction I had been able to give the team. I confirmed that we were willing to show good will and determination in bringing this to a close, and that if the Minister could resolve the remaining issues tomorrow, we could move on to discuss the arrangement for signing (a message meant to confirm our seriousness).

We spent most of our meeting discussing the four policy issues that Luong had presented on July 3. Luong was coming to understand our very real constraints, but we discussed formulations that could at least meet Vietnamese concerns part way.

The Ministers Meet, July 6

Charlene agreed to meet Minister Vu Khoan late in the morning of July 6. Khoan began thanking us for setting a very positive atmosphere the past few days, which he considered an encouraging signal. Khoan then affirmed that indeed the BTA was in the interest of both countries, and that its significance went beyond our bilateral relationship, being of importance to the entire region.

Now the suspense began: how much of the rest of the agreement's substance would he mentions as being necessary to negotiate? True to Luong's tip, Khoan focused almost exclusively on the telecommunications provisions, observing that the commitment to allow a 51% U.S. share in telecom joint ventures went beyond the commitments taken by China in the WTO. He explicitly requested that the maximum share for Americans now be limited to 49%.

Charlene's reply was brief. She thanked the Minister for his thorough presentation and affirmed that we were willing to listen and consider Vietnam's views. However, she noted that while her May 17 letter intended to demonstrate good will and understanding on our part to certain difficult issues to Vietnam, that it not mean that the United States was prepare to change its position from a year ago. She stopped here, saying that we would respond in the afternoon to each point he had raised. Khoan closed the session saying that Charlene had given him "some hope" that the U.S. would be flexible.

When we met again in the afternoon, I had reason to be optimistic: Vu Khoan had raised only one issue of any substantive difficulty for us, telecommunications, and Charlene, I could tell, was ready to deal on it in some fashion. She opened the afternoon session by seeking a critical clarification: she asked the Minister point blank if he had authorization to sign a final agreement here in Washington. Her fear was that we might make a concession, only to have Khoan say that he had to return to Hanoi to consult, after which Vietnam might move the goal post. Khoan replied that we could reach agreement on substance, he was empowered to sign it, though of course he would need consult with the Prime Minister on substance.

I felt this answer was sufficient, but Charlene was not satisfied. She felt the reply was still ambiguous, and asked to re-state the question. Once we reach agreement, are you authorized to sign it here, she asked. Vu Khoan replied simply, "Yes". Satisfied now, she continued: "I may have some flexibility in the context of a final signed agreement. Khoan confirmed:"I have made this clear. I expect to receive this flexibility".

Closing the deal, July 9-10

When Charlene and Vu Khoan met that Monday, I was hoping that the deal would be done. Charlene was prepared for one more fall back from our position on telecom – to offer the "Chinese" package on telecom (i.e., to allow only 49% U.S. participation for basic telecom services, albeit within the shorter time frame what we had already proposed).

Khoan then moved on to his instructions. He could accept the shorter time frames for transition proposed on telecommunications, he reported. Finally, he said he appreciated the possibility of more discussion on banking, and on textiles, noted that the appropriate time to begin negotiations of a quota agreement was after entry-into-force of the BTA.

Charlene responded by holding her ground. Charlene was going to play chicken with Vu Khoan, to see if he would retreat. She also had to push back on textiles as well, saying that the process of negotiations had to at least begin before Congress had approved the BTA. Vu Khoan remained calm and measured. "I appreciate your flexibility so far", he said, "but please think over our response today, and consider making an additional small step".

When the Ministers met the next morning, the air, for me at least, was charged with anticipation and excitement. Charlene asked Vu Khoan for his report and he repeated that Vietnam would be willing to accept equity terms in telecom modeled after China. In the spirit of flexibility, Charlene responded that upon reflection, and in view of the President's desire to complete the agreement, she would accept Vietnam's proposal.

The two Ministers shook hands, and four and a half years of negotiation effectively came to an end the morning of July 10, 2000, one day short of exactly five years since diplomatic relations were restored. Luong and I exchanged broad smiles. No one in room was more elated than the two of us.

Singing the Agreement

Charlene, who was in constant communication with the White House, confirmed that the President indeed wanted to announce the signing of the agreement. However, the President was at Camp David at the moment trying to broker peace in the Middle East, and we were going to have to wait until he returned to Washington. In the mean time, USTR was to make no announcement.

I quiet passed the word to a few insiders, such as Ginny Foote and Dan Price, but otherwise had to be coy with the press, which was starting to scent the story. I was glad in fact that we had some time to pore over the text again, finish the side letter, and I prepare press materials. The most time consuming of these was naturally the first, as there were still technical details to be worked out.

On the morning of July 13, they were to get together at about 10 at the Vietnam embassy. I was expecting that we would have the day to work through remaining issues and finalize the text. I learned quickly that we did not. Charlene called me to tell me that the White House had informed her that the President would announce the signing of the agreement *today* at 4 p.m.

I had a few hours to prepare the final versions of the texts in English and Vietnamese for signature by 3 p.m. so that the President could announce the signing at 4. The first thing I did was try to contact Rhonda at the Vietnamese embassy, something which it took me some time to do. Once I did, I told her that she had until noon at most to finish any final tweaks to the text, and then she had to return back to USTR to help print it out. I informed the Vietnamese of the signing as well.

The rest of the morning, I worked on finalizing briefing documents, press releases, and responding to a series of questions from our front office. I also had to arrange for a signing ceremony. We did not even have formal "signing" pens, we also had a problem with the treaty paper (according to the protocol office at the State Department), one in each language, and two on Vietnamese treaty paper. We had a ream of official treaty paper, but soon determined that it was not standard size 8½ by 11 inch paper, and so would not feed through our laser printer. We just had to spend time getting State Department to agree that it was "OK" to print the agreement on regular bond paper.

We had reached this point by noon. But I discovered that we did not have any bond paper either. Ginny Foote, who I had informed of the signing that morning, tried to help in this effort, but could not find enough at the stationary store near

USTR. I was determined that I had to run over to the nearest Staples (about 8 blocks away) to find the paper. On the way back, I received a phone call from Gene Sperling's office (Sperling was the President's International Economic Policy Advisor) telling me to go to the West Wing of the White House at 3.30 to brief the President on the agreement. Why weren't they calling Charlene, I thought. Nonetheless, I was very excited by the prospect to brief President Clinton.

Rhonda informed me that Luong insisted that Vietnam used its own treaty paper, even though it too was not standard size, and would not feed in a standard laser printer.

I ran over to the USTR annex building near 3 p.m to check on the arrangements for signing. The room was being set up. As 3 pm approached, Rhoda was just finishing a successful printing of the long text.

But Luong and his team were nowhere to be found. We learned, from the Vietnamese team who did show (including the Minister and Ambassador Le Van Bang), that they had had to go to Kinkos to print out the agreement in each language. As the minutes wound down, Nancy Leamond, who was the liaison with the White House, was getting increasingly agitated. We had to sign the agreement now, she instructed me. I passed this word to the Minister, but he would not budge. He wanted to wait for Luong – the man who had done all the work after all and the text on Vietnamese paper. It was unconscionable to this career diplomat that we could sign the biggest bilateral agreement between the United States and Vietnam since the end of the war, and do it both without the Vietnamese negotiators present, and just as importantly, not on Vietnamese paper and in Vietnamese.

Finally, Charlene broke the logjam, by proposing to Khoan personally that we would do a proper signing ceremony the following day —on proper paper, with toasts etc.,but that we need to sign some version of the agreement now, so that the President could say that it had been done in his remarks. This was an embarrassing moment, but Vu Khoan agreed. The two Ministers quickly sat down and signed the text on the U.S. paper, and in English only (we did not have software to print the Vietnamese version at USTR). Nancy told us we needed to hustle now to the White House, a block away.

But Luong was nowhere in sight still, and was now in danger of missing the entire White House ceremony. Vu Khoan was visibly upset, and I was mortified. It was a horrible scene. We began to walk slowly toward the White House. Just as we were about to enter the grounds, leaving Luong behind, his van came rolling down 17th Street, and he and Mr. Binh jumped out. He had made it with literally only seconds to spare. A red light on 17th Street would have made the difference.

The President of course spent his time conversing with Vu Khoan (who I could tell now was about elated as we were) about the historic significance of the event. After a few pleasantries, we were ushered out to the Rose Garden, where the press corps waited. The President made the announcement of the historic signing. I was amazed when the President thanked me by name in his remarks, in addition to Charlene and Richard.

The next morning, July 14, we staged our proper signing ceremony with Luong and his team. Luong and I initialed every page of both texts in both languages, followed by a signing by the Ministers and clinking of the champagne. Lots of pictures were taken, and this time, the private sector was invited in.

After the ceremony, Ginny has somehow miraculously arranged for a luncheon in the Ballroom at the Willard Hotel, and managed to get a couple of hundred people to show. Luong and I, with Ginny and Pete, Vu Khoan, Le Bang and a few of Ginny's board members, savored the moment at the head table. I gave a few remarks about the journey we had just completed, and how Luong and I had become friends. It was a moving moment for all of us, I think.

Coda

President Clinton indeed traveled to Vietnam in November, after the election (while it was still unclear who the victor would be, by the way). I was asked to come along. I was generally nowhere near the big events (those spots were reversed for the President's huge entourage and the many VIPs who had come along), but it was nonetheless gratifying that the BTA was the substantive centerpiece of his visit, and of his historic remarks at Hanoi University. I thought how lucky I was to have been involved in the project from beginning to end: it could not have ended on a much more dramatic note.

Trade negotiations don't often get to see the results of their work recognized in this way. The word "historic" is used liberally in Washington, especially by Presidents. But seeing the hoards of people lining the streets in Hanoi and Ho Chi Minh city – who showed up somehow on words of mouth (the

Government did not publicize his schedule), straining to see the man – brought home just how meaningful, how real, our achievement was. We had done something that would alter the troubled course of relations between our two countries for goods, and would re-make the face of Vietnam's economy. Beyond that, Luong and I had learned that with patience and understanding, despite the wide gulf of history and culture separating us, it was possible for the United States and Vietnam to understand each other.

(Excerpted from "Give Trade a Chance" book – Thế giới (The World) Publishers.

Translator: Quang Ha)

My July 13

"In that evening, I burned incense to my father, with respect and saying to him that: I could do the hardest thing in my life, I could accomplish the life's trials, and I was worthy to be yours" - Nguyen Dinh Luong

July 13, 2000 was the most memorable day in my life

The day when the Vietnam-U.S Trade Agreement was signed in Washington, the capital of the United States of America - a huge burden was lifted from my thin shoulders, after 5 years of wrestling.

My dream, my desire of having a legal document leveraging the pressure of time to eliminate the outdated and stagnant subsidized economic mechanism for the country to go forward, was fulfilled.

The day when I entered the White House, met and took photos with President Bill Clinton, and then received thanks from him as saying that "Thank you Vietnam's Chief negotiator Nguyen Dinh Luong" in a press release which was live broadcast by CNN, was watched by the whole world, including my wife and children at home.

To me, a plowman from Nghe An, a barren land of only stones and rocks, the result was noteworthy, I didn't dream anything more.

Today, July 13, 2020, after 20 years have elapsed, I recall happy and sad stories of that days.

Who and why decided July 13 for signing?

After signing the Minutes of agreement and principles in Hanoi on July 25, 1999; the Vietnam - US Trade Agreement had basically been completed. There were only 11 points, mainly technical, a few percent of opening services need further discussing. The two sides could have signed at the APEC Summit in Auckland (New Zealand, September 1999), but they missed the opportunity.

The Vietnamese negotiation delegation came to Washington DC on July 3, 2000 for a thorough preparation. Minister Vu Khoan arrived in a few days later.

He stayed with the Embassy. The negotiation delegation stayed at the motel, according to the Finance Ministry's spending ($20/day, of which a lunch meal cost $11).

After a courtesy meeting to introduce participants, it took only more than half an hour for two delegations of Vietnam and the United States to agree on issues, of which three ones were left to be handled at the ministerial level (increasing some percent of financial services and telecommunications).

Everything took place smoothly and favorably, and Joe Damond, the U.S chief negotiator and I discussed and consented to organize for having two ministers officially sign on July 11, 2000.

July 11, 2000 was also June 11 of lunar calendar, my father's passing away anniversary. To prepare myself for my father's passing away anniversary while I would be staying at

Washington, I brought with me incense with a plan to buy flowers to worship him. I would be very happy if the Agreement was signed on July 11.

However, on the morning of July 11, Damond quoted the White House to inform me that the Agreement was not about to be signed because the date and time of the ceremony would be decided by President.

In that evening, I burned incense to my father, with respect and saying to him that: I could do the hardest thing in my life, I could accomplish my life's trials, and I was worthy to be yours".

My father was an intelligent, talented, elegant and beloved man. He enthusiastically participated and was responsible in the work of union and revolution. I always followed his example. It's pity that he passed away too soon, in a difficult time, so, my mother and we had encountered many hardships.

Then, Damond told me that President had decided the date and time for signing because he wanted to be the first person to announce the world the signing of the first important agreement between the two former adversaries in reconciling spirit.

Later, I understood more why the agreement needed to be signed at 13:00, since President had a press conference at 14:00 where he addressed that "A few moments ago, Ambassador Barshefsky and Minister Vu Khoan signed an Agreement between the United States and Vietnam…"

Signing for pictures, official signing and two photos

As decided, at exactly 13:00 on July 13, the two delegations met to sign. But, the Vietnamese version was not available. Before leaving, the Ministry of Foreign Affairs thoroughly prepared the Agreement's cover, several hundred hard paper sheets with borders, papers for Vietnamese Agreements.

From the early morning of July 13, Lawyer Nguyen Hong Duong, who was in charge of the agreement's documents found a place to print, but, there was not any place to print hard papers. Finally, the Agreement was printed from the disc onto the U.S white paper and then captured. A total of 300 sheets in both Vietnamese and English version were printed in such way. The process could not be finished within a morning. Lawyer Duong printed the Agreement. I stayed at home to handle the arising matters.

At that time, two ministers, two ambassadors and members of the delegations, journalists had to wait for so long…

It was time to go to the White House to meet President, Minister Vu Khoan and Ambassador Barshefsky sat at the table, held pens in hand with the two Ambassadors standing behind, as , photos were taken.

That was only "photoshoot signing ceremony" and the pictures of signing were also photoshoots but July 13 was recorded in the Agreement as the signing date.

The two sides made an appointment of meeting each other at 10 am on July 14. Joe Damond and I initialed every page, each person needed to initial nearly 600 signatures. Then two ministers officially signed and took photos, constituting the properly official signing ceremony. Photos of official signing ceremony which featured two ministers, two ambassadors and two chief negotiators were taken.

Getting in and out of the White House

Again I will discuss our going to the White House. When it was time to go to the White House to meet President Bill Clinton, I was still preparing the Agreement, while people became impatient and were urged to leave, but Minister Vu Khoan was determined to find Luong, and only when Luong got into the car did he set off.

Fortunately, I returned in time, and was really grateful for Minister's delicate attitude. He was indeed an excellent and wonderful diplomat.

Passing through security station, we were taken to the Roosevelt room where important U.S officials such as Ambassador Barshefsky, Senator John McCain, Senator John Kerry, Representative Reyes, Under Secretary of State for Economic Affair Larson, Ambassador Peterson and the U.S Chief Negotiator Joe Damond were present.

While everyone was waiting, at the White House's Rose Garden, the helicopter carrying President Bill Clinton landed. He, had just returned from Camp David where he was holding talks between Israel and Palestine. He gladly shook hands with each person and took pictures with Minister Vu Khoan and some others.

After a few minutes of greeting and intimately talking, everyone went to the Rose Garden to attend the press conference which was broadcast live by CNN. President delivered a speech, briefing on the normalization process of the U.S-Vietnam relations; process of searching for the Bilateral Trade Agreement to be signed, the Agreement's significances to Vietnam's socio-economic development; and he concluded his speech by saying: "This agreement is one more reminder that the former adversaries can come together to find a common ground in a way of benefits for the peoples, to let go over the past and embrace the future, to forgive and to reconcile". He also extended thanks to contributors to the success of this negotiation.

When President said: "Thank you Vietnam's chief negotiator Nguyen Dinh Luong", Joe Damond standing next to me pinched my hands, two of us looked at each other and happily smiled.

After getting out of the White House's security station for ten steps, Minister Vu Khoan slowed down, put his arm around my shoulder, it seemed important and he whispered "Luong, there is one thing that I now dare to say: Cam called me that once the Agreement is signed, you need to come back immediately to report to the Politburo, everyone is waiting...". I was the person who grasped all issues of the Agreement, so, it was correct that I needed to come back for report. But honestly, I wanted to have a few days relaxing after such a time of hard work.

Then I clicked my tongue: My fate is miserable. Great poet Nguyen Du has said:" Đã mang lấy nghiệp vào thân, cũng đừng trách lẫn trời gần trời xa" (How hard you work is God gave you to do, just don't complain to the Sky close or far)

Luckily, I couldn't get a ticket right away, as getting a ticket from Vietnam to the U.S at that time was not like today.

The most delicious Vodka in my life

After the Agreement was signed on July 14, the Minister returned to the Vietnamese Embassy. As it was not time to prepare for dinner, the delegation came to the Trade Office.

I felt really strange and indescribably comfortable at that time, may be it was the joy of the fact that burden was lifted. Suddenly, I had a flat feeling in mouth and wanted a strong drink, but did not know which it was.

Luckily, when glancing at the bookshelf, I found a bottle of Vodka, my eyes became bright, here it was, exactly what I wanted. The bottle was immediately opened, each person had a cup and drank in one go. Oh my God, how delicious it was, so cool. That feeling was like one of a plowman having finished work amidst the blazing and unforgiving sun, getting a rest and taking a puff of pipe tobacco deeply and released smoke into the sky. Ecstatic!

Joe Damond, close friend Ginny Foote and I had plan to meet each other on July 13, 2020 for a gala organized to celebrate the 20th anniversary of signing the Agreement. Everything seemed to be fine, but the resurgence of the Covid-19 forced the gala to be scrapped. We had to accept. That was our fate.

And perhaps I will find it difficult to return to Washington DC again to meet my friends because I am older, weaker and planning to return back my hometown for an idyllic life with bamboo, paddy fields, and scorching Lao winds.

Three reasons for successful signing of the U.S – Vietnam BTA Agreement

"The first and foremost important reason was that negotiators of Vietnam and the United States could build mutual trust and sympathy".

Joseph Damond - The U.S Chief negotiator

(Cited from an article published on the Saigon Times - January 2001)

The greatest impression about the agreement negotiation process was that the two sides with little understanding on each other as the process started, had learned how to work well with each other to build mutual trust and sympathy.

When I first came to Vietnam in late 1995 (which was the first visit of U.S trade officials to Hanoi), we knew very little about the Vietnam's trading system, laws and procedures. I supposed that the Vietnamese side had also little understanding of the U.S system and regulations, standards of the World Trade Organization (WTO) on which my country's trading system was based. Through an elaborate process of researching, we soon realized that our systems were largely different.

Our common task, as I identified it at the time, was seeking ways to harmonize the two different systems. Fortunately, Vietnam was determined to move forwards to the WTO standards recognized by most countries in the world, including ASEAN member countries.

Because the trade ties between the United States and most nations were based on WTO's and international standards, we believed that in order to establish long-term, solid and really "normalized" trade relations with Vietnam, the Agreement must be based on these standards. Obviously, this was not always easy for Vietnam, a country which was still in economic transition.

However, step by step, we found ways to move forwards. The Vietnamese side studied more closely about how other developing countries had adopted WTO's and international standards into their systems. The U.S side learned about the reality in Vietnam and saw difficulties that this country was facing in the transition and how it made efforts to overcome. One thing that I thought both sides could feel was that such a trade agreement was a win-win situation. During the process of negotiating trade agreement, both sides implemented on the basis of mutual benefits.

In my opinion, there were three reasons why we could complete the Agreement: Firstly, Vietnam acknowledged benefits and the need of applying a WTO-based trading system. Secondly, the United States, once it realized that Vietnam needed time to apply this system as it was new, was flexible in negotiation. But, the first and foremost reason was that negotiators of Vietnam and the United States could build mutual trust and sympathy. I had a great admiration for my counterpart Nguyen Dinh Luong. Over time, I had not only learned how to thoroughly understand his vision and delegation but I also had a trust in his words. I believed he would also learn how to understand my vision and have a trust in me. Despite the wide gulf of viewpoints and stances separating us, we both found responsible and possible to find ways for understanding each other.

The BTA and the thick shroud of smoke of war

"It took a long time for Vietnam to believably consider the U.S proposal. The U.S side said that the Agreement would bring benefits to both sides, but perhaps, some Vietnamese people supposed that we were bluffing"

Phuong Loan (Vietnamnet - 2010)

"Please don't talk about it, what a painful thing", that was an initial reply that the writer received. After much persuasion, the writer got a nod to recreate hardships of opening the Vietnam- U.S trade door, of erecting a bridge between the two former enemies.

Turning over pages full of words in a black, blue and small notebook, tears fell from the smiling eyes of experienced speaker Nguyen Dinh Luong. "This is the notebook of his life. With this small notebook, he delivered many speeches themed "the Vietnam-U.S Trade Agreement is a specific product of the specific relationship between Vietnam and the United States" from the central to provincial and city levels. Read it to understand and penetrate," he said.

Fifteen years ago, the two nations' speakers entered the negotiations with a gulf between two sides due to "an unforgettable war in the past, unconfident present and uncertain future".

Not as easy as Eastern European countries when negotiating BTAs with the United States, considering a BTA as a must-have passport to seize opportunities joining the EU, NATO, also unlike some other countries considering BTA signing and accepting US's access their markets as a chance for national rapid development, Vietnam had its own circumstances, intentions and negotiating principles; besides, it has to surmount its own specific obstacles.

Together, the past, present and future were an are enormous-obstacle and burden on the negotiation process of the Vietnam-U.S BTA from the very beginning. And, first of all, that derived from the smoke shaded by a brutal war the United States made in Vietnam.

Haunted by the war

October 1995, just three months after the two countries pronounced the normalization of diplomatic relations, on the occasion of attending a United Nations meeting, Foreign Minister Nguyen Manh Cam and the U.S Trade Representative agreed to launch BTA negotiations to finalize the full normalization of relations between the two countries.

Earlier, Vietnam advocated for the diversification and multilateralization of international relations, and was willing to make friends with other nations for peace and development.

However, that did not mean negotiation would be a smooth sailing, and few words would not suffice for shaking hands

A series of obstacles stood in the way for the society and people of both sides. They needed to be put aside first.

Unlike previous negotiations between Vietnam and the United States, this negotiation aimed to build a long-term partnership. Negotiation must be based on understanding and trust. However, Vietnam's chief negotiator admitted that "at the time when starting to negotiate with the United States, I myself didn't have that".

"The war inflicted pain to my whole family. Our generation is loyal to the implementation of Uncle's Ho teachings: Đánh cho Mỹ cút... (Beating the United States to get out of the country)".

Hence, even though the war ended, hatred of the United States still exists, even deeply. On the first trip to the United States, Director General of the General Department of Post Office Mai Liem Truc shuddered when traversing the Pentagon, the White House headquarters...And that was not just his personal feeling.

Vietnam's history was associated with wars, but there had never been a war as devastating as one that the United States waged in Vietnam, with millions of tons of bombs and bullets dropped the country. Not a single city in Vietnam remained intact. Not a single village was not full of bomb craters. Not a single family, both in the North and South, on one side and the other side that did not experienced pain caused by the war.

The war not only caused pain to Vietnamese, but it was also a "political headache for the United States", said Virginia Foote, President of the U.S- Vietnam Trade Council, who practiced a shuttle diplomacy between the two countries during years of negotiations. "The issue related to the war still hovers in the United States... There are politicians, congressmen and residents who don't want to normalize relations with Vietnam."

Many Americans are "still annoyed and angry about the past". The war with Vietnam has remained a burning controversy in the United States. American veterans feel bad, some reckoned that Americans withdrew too soon, others said America withdrew too late...

That the two sides have such feelings is understandable, according to Luong. The United States' history was associated with constant wars, but it had never lost against any nation. The United States only lost in Vietnam War in the time when it was the most powerful country in the world and the White House's will of destroying Vietnam's patriotic movements was the highest in its history. The failure made the whole United States stunned, lose direction and feel guilty. It also shattered Americans' pride in American values.

"The war became a torment in the heart of the U.S politics."

Joseph Damond, the U.S chief negotiator, also admitted that "some of the U.S congressmen and citizens criticize and don't believe in the normalization. Although they are a minority, they sometimes cause noise and psychological disturbance".

On the first time of coming to the United States to attend an exhibition of Vietnamese goods in San Francisco in 1994 summer, Luong "felt very strange" as hearing overseas Vietnamese shouting "Down with Viet Cong!" from morning to night. Sitting in a bulletproof Cadillac car, he found chicken egg and duck eggs were thrown at him outside the car.

"Even now, there are still people who don't want to develop relations with Vietnam, stating that the United States was so hasty in normalizing the ties. They don't want to get involved, don't want the United States to do anything with Vietnam, though they are just a minority", said Foote.

For both sides, "it was an unforgettable war". "Pain caused by the war and heaviness of the post-war pressure didn't make the negotiation's atmosphere an easy one and they kept heavily weighing on negotiators' shoulders of both sides", Luong said.

Overwhelming suspicion

Haunted by the unforgettable war, everything was covered by the suspicion mentally.

The war was so cruel and painful that it made Vietnamese people feel reluctant to hear about America coming back to this strip of land.

At that time, America was considered as "fundamental and long term enemy" in Vietnamese people's eyes. Anti-American sentiment soaked into the subconscious mind of all social classes. Their thinking and attitude to Americans, despite bilateral diplomatic relation normalization, were still keeping their guard against and enemy, known as "always take our fighting attitude against the stubborn enemy".

Moreover, the ideological difference furthermore heightened the suspicion. It was still difficult to accept doing business with the former foe. Especially, when the Vietnamese mind was still obsessed by Kissinger's words: "Americans who did not win the war will win the peace".

"Vietnam had to spend too much time deciding whether to believe what the Americans proposed. The US side always said that the Agreement would bring benefits to both sides, but perhaps, some people in Vietnam speculated that we were bluffing," US Chief negotiator Joe Damond said in retrospect.

Therefore, the BTA was "both opposed by many people with criticism and supported by a lot of others", but few spoke up to probably protect themselves", Luong once said.

They were suspicious, raised questions and they used the word "conspiracy" for American intentions in BTA.

The BTA used to be considered as a "scheme of transform Vietnam's political regime". Also, it was simply supposed to be a "conspiracy of destroying the socialism", "breaking the socialist-oriented economy". The suspicion occurred over all parts of the agreement, to every article's content, every sentence, every words…

Those supporting the BTA themselves felt cautious of being asked about their class stance.

""BTA is a bone that is both big and hard, neither be swallowed nor be chewed," Luong compared.

Enlightened by the national interests

Therefore, the 5-year negotiation put the diplomat Nguyen Dinh Luong and the Vietnamese negotiation delegation under pressure, and was as stressful as a high-wire performance in circus, on the thin line between merit and delinquency, sometimes seeming be so much exhausted as to fall down. "Actually, both opposers and supporters showed their patriotism based on their own ways, thinking, awareness and vision ", Mr. Luong mused.

Though it was very hard in the mind games to convincing one's negotiating partners, it could not be compared with each negotiator's efforts to overcome himself, and find his domestic consensus and approval.

Originating the initial hatred against the US, "gradually, I understand what this Vietnamese nation, this country of Vietnamese needs from me is not the hatred of the US, but overcoming my own psychological and social barriers to create a national once-in-a-lifetime opportunity. What needs to be done must be completed and done till the end", Mr. Luong confided.

Arriving in Quang Nam to speak in front of hundreds of people, including many veterans, about the Trade Agreement at a newly built, both large and beautiful Tam Ky Hall, Luong asked to light incense sticks to pray for Vietnamese descendants who shed their blood for the country's independence and said that the merits of the heroic martyrs, the heroic Vietnamese mothers were forever memorized deeply in mind by the nation. And to pray to them to "bless this country to stand up holding the head high, not to let poverty and backwardness make kneeling down. Because a country holding a grudge forever can make itself sick and weak to rise up."

"It was extremely difficult to speak face to face between the two sides without motivation enlightened by the very strong light – light of national, country's interests".

Starting from deeply separating gaps which seemed be impossible to fill, the two sides together made equal efforts of "picking up small stones to fill the gaps, taking carefully each needle to untangle a perplexed thread", so that on July 13, 2000, the two countries signed the BTA to fully complete the normalization process, opening a new chapter in two countries' relations, normalizing not only politics.

Vietnam - U.S BTA and the journey of learning mutual understanding

"The advantage was that we soon realized both sides were really willing to learn and approach the negotiation with trust and frankness, so we could learn to trust each other."

Phuong Loan (Vietnamnet – July 6th, 2010)

"I was aware that the gulf between our expectations and objectives was huge" for the BTA, because the US and Vietnam have had few negotiations in the past on economy and, trade" Joe Damond said in retrospect when he was appointed to be Chief Negotiator of US negotiation delegation.

The two countries' approaches to trade agreements were very different at the time. US trade agreements are based on WTO rules, which seemed be still very new to Vietnam.

Breaking barriers by avoiding capitalist rules

In fact, before embarking on the negotiation, Vietnam submitted to join GATT - the predecessor of the WTO from the end of 1994, in which it pledged that Vietnam would strictly implement GATT regulations for being admitted by the organization. And, from January 3, 1995, when the WTO was born, Vietnam joined the organization as its observer.

"Though we did make such a desire and commitment, we didn't understand WTO rules", said Nguyen Dinh Luong. "The experts in the Vietnamese negotiating team all experienced a lot in BTA negotiations, but they were trained in the former Soviet Union and Eastern Europe, and the concept of the World Trade Organization (WTO) seemed to be still new to them."

"Our habit and custom of living and working did not follow the capitalism's law, the logic of legal thinking was still basically simple, and had long shunned the rules of the capitalist market..."

Therefore, the alienation from the rules of the capitalist game and refusal to approach the other world's way of doing business made Vietnamese negotiators found it unheard-of to accept the WTO's regulations as a common game rule for the Vietnam-US BTA negotiation.

"At the start of the negotiation, we looked for a teacher to learn but could neither find any in Vietnam nor in our "brother nations" due to different national philosophies," said Luong. "The WTO rules had not yet reached Vietnam, we had not approached, of course impossibly applied".

Moreover, the Vietnam's economic system was completely different from the world's. That was a state-owned, monopolistic economy. At that time, import and export were absolutely operated by the state. Concepts such as equality between domestic and foreign goods, between national and foreign enterprises in the game of the capital rules were found too strange to Vietnam. Some even thought that it had been a US conspiracy to destroy Vietnam's socialist economy.

"The National Treatment principle has been even included in GATT since 1947, but it was not translated correctly into Vietnamese, sometimes was "đối xử quốc dân" 'domestic treatment'?, or "đối xử công dân" (citizen treatment)…and finally " đối xử quốc gia" (national treatment).

"In the beginning, Vietnam has a lot to learn and many steps to take before it can be ready to join GATT/WTO," said Joe Damond.

Unable to find an expert for teaching, the Vietnamese negotiating delegation had to "wrestle themselves" with the WTO rules. By downloading documents on the Internet, negotiators assigned each other to read, analyze, process... and then submit.

Many seminars and training programs had been held for Vietnam to study other countries' experience which aimed to help Vietnam understand the WTO and the benefits and difficulties of integration.

Vietnam – US, searching for mutual understanding and trust

Not only was it unfamiliar with the new rules of the WTO, but Vietnam also found the US a completely new type of negotiating partner. Despite his 20 year experience in negotiating bilateral trade agreements, Mr. Nguyen Dinh Luong mainly negotiated with partners of socialist countries, on the basis of comradeship, the same economic institutions, same economic system, a similar legal system... even newcomers such as Singapore, Switzerland, Norway, Canada... "but they were not America".

"We didn't understand anything about the United States, but were just aware that it would be very difficult to negotiate with the US. The world super powers such as Europe, Japan, and China have to still consider the US a redoubtable partner", Mr. Luong said.

Encouraged by the mindset "Success is unexpected without well understanding partner", Mr. Nguyen Dinh Luong and the negotiating delegation looked for books on the US... "Everything started to roughly appear. When I felt that I understood the basic features of the US and WTO, I gradually rekindled the hope of possibly speaking on a par with the US", Mr. Luong once confided on Investment Newspaper.

Indeed, both sides mainly wanted to understand mutual thinking for the first meeting and discussions.

"The initial rounds of negotiations were mainly to listen to the US side's explanations, suggesting them to talk as much as possible, to clearly understand the partners' goals, intentions, and requirements," Mr. Luong said.

Joe Damond, the US chief negotiator, said that the negotiators' first meetings were essentially the two sides' "struggling to understand each other". "Honestly, in the first few years, we weren't always successful."

The US side knew too little about Vietnam's trade system and its rules, therefore, it took many questioning sessions and learning about the Vietnam's systems.

Similarly, the Vietnamese side had many questions about the US trade system, trade law and US trade policy, making the US negotiators take a lot of time to explain them.

""We could only design and build our plans basing on a thorough understanding, when we had not fully searched for additional knowledge yet, no matter what the criticizing or disparaging", said Luong .

"We took advantage of soon realizing that both sides were really willing to learn and approach negotiations with trust and frankness, so that we could learn to trust each other," said Joe Damond in retrospect. The atmosphere on the negotiating table, especially between Mr Joe Damond and his peer, Mr. Luong, had never been angry or bitter.

"I believe we both take a responsibility of doing this job best to possibly benefit both sides, even if it was very difficult at the time," said Joe Damond.

"It was very clear that Vietnam wanted to ensure that the proposals made by the United States also serve Vietnam's national benefits," he added. "I highly appreciated that. I also knew it wouldn't be easy for Vietnam to accept our interpretation, but you need to understand the US proposal deeply and then make your decision."

In the summer of 1998, "we managed to control the situation by completing the draft created by the Vietnamese side and after being approved, the negotiating delegation gave it to the US side in the fifth round of negotiations for the first time in Washington DC," Mr. Luong said in retrospect.

From "Vietnam knew little about the trade agreement that the US was aiming for", according to Joe Damond, "through negotiations, Vietnam had learned very quickly".

"We are so surprised at the progress of the Vietnamese delegation... Negotiating with a partner like you, we find it interesting," said the Chief negotiator of the US delegation in the first substantive discussion, after Vietnam handed over the draft.

In fact, it is the product of the process of "research to understand the US, understand the American people, country, society, research to understand what is the current world like, how the WTO rules are, then calculate the benefits Vietnam gains in this game", as Chief negotiator of the Vietnamese Negotiating Delegation, Mr. Nguyen Dinh Luong, said.

"Once I visualized Vietnam's interests, I realize that our path is very straight: this country's interest is to sign the BTA with the US, because without signing, it was impossible to integrate into the world. That's the only path to develop."

Mr. Luong added, "The BTA negotiation with the US is to build a long-term business partnership. The partnership of a long-lasting cooperation must base on mutual trust, and no ground for quickie, snatched playing. The mutual trust must set up from both two sides' frankness, honesty but not naïve one."

Vietnamese side was always willing to frankly state the differences for the US to understand, when distance appeared between the two sides with the country's conditions. When we spoke reasonably and rationally, the US side always responded properly.

"After a lot of dialogues, discussions, some compromises of the US side, the Vietnamese side found us more trustworthy, and that makes Vietnam realize the agreement is meant to strengthen, not weaken the economy. In short, it was a great success of wise and respectful dialogue about feelings and suspicion," said Joe Damond.

The BTA and the missed opportunity

"Some people said Vietnam made a mistake, others said that missing (the BTA opportunity) was due to the US, but I think both sides had to pay too high a price. I always say that we have to compare two sides of a coin for an opened or closed door to our relationship"

Phuong Loan (Vietnamnet - July 8, 2010)

It took 4 years of negotiation, going through three Vietnamese Trade Ministers; Vietnam and the United States had almost reached a final agreement until it was suddenly "braked". That was in September 1999.

Personal belongings and documents were already in the suitcase, just waiting for orders; Chief negotiator of Vietnamese negotiating delegation for BTA Nguyen Dinh Luong and his delegation were going to New Zealand to finalize the negotiation and to participate in the signing of the official agreement as planned.

On the other side of the world, the 7th APEC Meeting had started; Mr. Luong's telephone was ringing continuously. International reporters called to hunt for the BTA information.

"Thank you for answering the phone," a reporter calling from abroad told him. "I call just to confirm if you have flown to New Zealand or are sitting there. Now you are answering the phone, I know that there won't be any signing in New Zealand."

Two months earlier, on July 25, 1999, for the first time after the four-year negotiation, the two sides issued a press release that Vietnamese and American negotiators had reached a basic agreement on the Bilateral Trade Agreement's principles. The Agreement deals with issues related to trade in goods, trade in services, protection of intellectual property rights, and investment relations between the two countries.

The signing was supposed to take place when the two sides met soon after for technical details to be agreed and have the Government and competent authorities consider its submission. In fact, the two sides had only 10-12 points for further discussion at that time, which were said by Mr Nguyen Dinh Luong and Ms. Virginia Foote to be very small and mostly technical issues.

The two sides could have hoped and should have agreed on the signing in Auckland, New Zealand in September 1999, on the occasion of the APEC Conference when both the US President and Vietnamese Prime Minister were present, witnessed and remembered by the whole world at this important event.

"The signing should have been in New Zealand in an international conference, and the two countries would have set a background to propagate the Agreement normalizing the economic and trade relations between the two former foes. US President Bill Clinton would have made his mark in history as the person who closed the Vietnam page for the whole world to witness. And in that November, the US Congress would have quickly passed it to keep up with President Clinton's Asia trip, in which Vietnam had been one of the stops", Mr. Nguyen Dinh Luong analyzed.

"Moreover, the Americans also wanted to take advantage of the BTA with Vietnam to signal China, who was in tough negotiations with the US on the WTO that the US was capable to sign with such a hard-to-deal-with partner as Vietnam"

"Its prosperity was very bright and full of optimism," Virginia Foote said in retrospect.

"I thought we could go faster to finish the negotiation process," said Joe Damond, chief US negotiator.

Unfortunately, "in the end, the two sides did not reach to the signing". "Vietnam's fortunate opportunity has not come yet," regretted Nguyen Dinh Luong.

The failure of signing in New Zealand "stressed everyone angrily and frustratedly," Ms. Foote remembered feeling at the time. "We wondered what Vietnam really wanted, if you truly wanted to promote the normalization of economic relations between our two countries." "Clearly, Vietnam believed the country needed more time to study and review the agreement, so we had not been able to conclude the signing until July 2000. We wasted several months," said Joe.

"I was disappointed because the agreement took us a lot of effort and the US side did not know when Vietnam wanted to end this negotiation process."

In the following months, the two sides hardly had any dialogue or contact, except for the personal contact between Virginia Foote and the Vietnamese Chief negotiator Nguyen Dinh Luong. All exchanges were suspended. The US negotiating delegation was ordered not to discuss with Vietnam about anything.

Those months of dialogue - cease created time for Vietnam once again to internally exchange, discuss, and clarify issues still raising troubles and questions.

Earlier in January 2000, the Vietnamese side agreed to continue the negotiation for signing. The US still kept their silent order of not having any discussion.

"It took a few months for the situation to improve; the two countries came together around the negotiating table and almost one year was taken, in July 2000, for the agreement to be signed," Virginia Foote remembered.

But anyway, Vietnam had missed the early fortune boat to open an equal playing field with the US.

"Near the end, we missed the opportunity and then lost the period of time wasted for an unworthy reason of its importance to the Vietnamese economy as well as to the American business community" Virginia Foote once said.

Virginia Foote was not randomly making such a statement, because the remaining gaps between the two countries were only minor, which were later resolved easily.

10 years have gone by, in retrospect of that missed opportunity, Joe Damond said, "We should have been aware of the unprecedented level and nature of the BTA to find it unsurprising for Vietnam's extending more a few months to fully consider it."

And, Virginia Foote said in retrospect, after Auckland, that Vietnam may have been right. What you asked for had not been achieved in Auckland but has been achieved in the final Agreement.

"In the negotiations, neither side was completely wrong, but, the mistake missing the boat, perhaps was made by the US more due to our over stubborness," said Virginia Foote.

Nonetheless, as the Vietnam's Chief negotiator taking key responsibility for negotiating, Mr. Nguyen Dinh Luong still felt "painful" because of the missed boat.

"If the signing had occurred earlier, in September 1999, Vietnam would have become a potentially attractive investment market to the US and the world. Only a few months late did provide China an adequate opportunity of reaching an agreement with the US for joining the WTO and that 1.3-billion-people market became the most attractive investment market in the world," Mr. Luong said.

However, Mr. Luong mused, "The mindset of change is not as immediate as you expect, not as easy to do as you talk. Changes only take shape in the process of self-awareness through books and practices, to observe the evolution of the times. Times change, we have to change too, tightly clinging to our very old ones can only harm ourselves."

Light of national benefits and the "stubborn"

"The pathway for us to go forward to the normalization of economic relations with the United States and then join the WTO is the right way for our country to escape poverty, backwardness and evolve with the times".

Phuong Loan (Vietnamnet - July 10, 2020)

There was a huge burden on negotiators, sadness, pain, and disappointment due to invisible pressures and tangible failures of the missed New Zealand opportunity, but, thanks to the light of national benefits and the "stubborn" refusingal to give up, the two countries had reached the final stage on the path of achieving BTA.

"Despite many difficulties, we have always made efforts to promote economic normalization with Vietnam", because "it is beneficial for both countries", Virginia Foote explained.

When the Vietnam-US BTA's signing in New Zealand was delayed, it disappointed the Americans, leading them to ask dubious questions about Vietnam's goodwill. When would Vietnam be ready? What did Vietnam really want?

"However, it's important that we didn't give up." "We had managed to get through that difficult year together," said Virginia Foote in retrospect.

She continued her shuttle diplomacy efforts, when the official dialogue channel between two countries' Governments was suspended. Meeting with Vietnamese partners to find out where the issues were, what to do to go forward, meeting the US side to convince them... That American woman constantly traveled back and forth between the two countries Vietnam - US, in the absence of direct principal-to-principal contact for communication and exchange.

"When it's broken, both sides need time to debate on how to recover it... We tried to figure out what the issue was, how to go forward..." When she was asked what made her, an American overcome   her disappointment of Vietnam's decision and not give up, Virginia Foote replied: "The two countries have gone a long way together, our destination could be seen too close. We have seen them, envisioned them, felt them and know how to overcome them. There's no reason to stop all these efforts we have made."

"The American controversy over the Vietnam War in the past did not prevent us from raising another question: whether it'd be better to build a relationship with today's Vietnam. What the Americans were effortfully doing was to make a debate on Vietnam of the future," she explained.

There were opponents, but many Americans recognized that Vietnam was an integral part of the America's regional strategy. Vietnam has already been a member of ASEAN, which the US couldn't have fully developed a regional strategy without. Vietnam is the 13th largest market in the world, with great business potential. There were already been businesses interested in and operating in Vietnam. Many veterans also wanted to put an end to the traumatic past of the war. It is better to make friends with Vietnam than remain an enemy of Vietnam.

Therefore, she and her colleagues actively sought out to understand Vietnam, and support Vietnam to understand the US and rules of the game in today's world.

Regarding Joe Damond, "I was very honored to be assigned the role of chief negotiator, because it would be an historic milestone". Joe was aware of the difficult and challenging negotiations right from the beginning and he always worked with the Vietnamese partner in dealings together to reach a consensus.

"We really wanted to set up the foundation to improve commercial relations and investment between the two countries. It meant that we needed something in return for lowering the average US import tariff and move Vietnam toward adoption of the WTO and other international trade and investment norms;" said Mr. Joe Damond.

The White House demanded him to promote a successful agreement, and he did it, after 5 years of negotiation, experiencing 11 rounds...

On the Vietnamese side, Nguyen Dinh Luong once prayed to heroes and martyrs in Quang Nam for the nation to hold its head high without bowing down due to hunger, poverty, and suffering; he reminded himself to "stand-up-straight" in facing difficulties when working as a negotiator.

"National interests, national benefits, development benefits required us to stand up straight, helped give us more courage, and forced us to be wise," Mr. Luong concluded.

"The path we take, towards normalizing economic relations with the US and then joining the WTO is the right path for our country to escape poverty, backwardness and evolve with the times."

Therefore, he clearly defined his and his comrades' task as entrusted by the country: to successfully negotiate an agreement in which both sides together benefited, for the establishment of trade cooperation relations with the US, paving the way for Vietnam's economy to take off and open the door to enter the WTO later.

"The BTA will also be the foundation for Vietnam to renew itself, speeding up the Doi Moi process that the Government has outlined since 1986."

The difficult and heavy responsibilities of the 5 year negotiation was a burden on Nguyen Dinh Luong and the Vietnamese delegation making them so exhausted as to nearly collapse on the negotiating table, but, "I always keep on faith of myself".

Sometimes, he felt that "how hard he was", but the initial results of negotiation were his "happy" motivation for him never giving up. That was the joy of designing the 5 principles of negotiation with the US for the Prime Minister to approve, and high-level approval; the joy after the time of plowing, digging up legal documents, comparing international commitments , the US's request for the Vietnamese legal system to make the BTA parallel draft, including a chapter provisionally rewritten by Vietnam itself. And the greatest joy was "removing the enormous burden", reconciling the painful pages of Vietnam - US history, when together with his American counterpart, Joe Damond, initialed 1,200 signatures on every page of the Agreement! Breathing a sign of relief like a farmer who has just finished a hard row to hoe.

On the date the two countries signed the Agreement, the American woman Virginia Foote went to a quiet corner, trying to hide her tears of joy rolling down the beaming-smiling face.

The day before that, at his hotel room in Washington DC, Mr. Nguyen Dinh Luong, on the occasion of the passing-away anniversary of his father, quietly lit incense brought from Vietnam to pray for his late father, who gave him his brain to participate in an "intellectual battle" with the Americans, and told his father: "This life's trials, I have accomplished".

The Agreement "opened a new page in the relationship between the two countries and left the painful past behind," said Joe Damond. "Honestly, I'm more proud to be a part of this achievement than anything else I've done in my career."

The light of national interests brought the Vietnamese and Americans closer together, becoming friends. Their journey was not only in those 5 years.

At the end of the signing, Virginia Foote and her colleagues continued their mobilizing journey for the US Congress to pass the Agreement with a majority of yes votes, so that American businesses could come and stay in Vietnam, not just "reserve a seat"…

And "ploughman" Nguyen Dinh Luong has not himself relaxed; together with his "life memorial book" he has gone to make presentations everywhere, but first of all, to "break the secret" of the Agreement, for Vietnamese people to really understand and potentially applying BTA, with hope that Vietnamese businesses will reap the sweet fruits growing from the first furrows plowed by those undertaking an arduous journey.

After 10 years, the BTA has been bringing many benefits to both sides.

Today, Vietnam and the United States celebrated 15 years of establishing diplomatic relations. In the memory of the US Ambassador to Vietnam Michael Michalak, the 15-year bilateral relations have achieved many good results, especially cooperation in economy - trade through the implementation of the Bilateral Trade Agreement. He also makes a prediction that, "there will be many positive results in further promoting multifaceted relations between the two countries". And "the United States completely shares common interests with Vietnam in terms of peace and stability in the region".

Nguyen Dinh Luong, a retired old man, who is enjoying a peasant's quiet and peaceful life, is still profound: "After completing the normalization process with the US and joining the WTO, Vietnam is like a vehicle entering a major road, facing others going both in the same and in the opposite direction, the driver must be conscious to drive it, his eyes must be sharp, with nice wheelman skill, to avoid accidents".

From burning tea cup to embarrassing negotiation for both sides

"The 30-year war and its fierceness had left too many problems in Vietnam and in Vietnam-US relations.

Huynh Phan (Vietnamnet - 2011)

- How did you become the chief negotiator?

- On the morning of November 5, 1996, at a meeting to prepare for economic and trade negotiations with the United States, after the relevant ministries and branches reported the situation, Deputy Prime Minister in charge of foreign economic affairs Tran Duc Luong, the chairperson, decided to set up the "Inter-ministerial working group on Economic - Trade Agreement with the United States".

Suddenly, he pointed at me, and said: "I decide to appoint comrade Nguyen Dinh Luong as the group's leader". I was really taken aback, and didn't have time to react, because he was so determined.

In my heart, I understood why he chose me. It was because I escorted him many times in negotiations or meetings of the Intergovernmental Committee with the Soviet Union and other socialist states. He comprehended what I was thinking and could do.

Since then, work related to negotiations between Vietnam and the United States was assigned to me to assemble and synthesize. When the U.S delegation arrived, I led the Vietnamese negotiating delegation.

- Joe Damond said that he was lucky because his boss proactively stepped aside, otherwise...

- I was not lucky like that. My fate was bad. "Đã mang lấy nghiệp vào thân/ Cũng đừng trách lẫn trời gần trời xa". (How hard you work is what God gave you to do, it doesn't matter what reasons you have to complain about" or don't complain to the Sky close or far.

- Joe Damond said that in the beginning, the U.S side was quite confused in conducting negotiations as they had little information and understanding of the Vietnamese economic and trade mechanism. And he also saw the same things from the Vietnamese side, didn't he?

- Both right and not right. It was right because we also didn't understand about the trade system of the United States and the world in general, apart from our socialist side.

Not right because the task for Vietnam was far more strenuous than for the U.S side. We not only didn't understand the U.S side but we also encountered other problems which needed to be handled while negotiating.

The 30-year-long war and its fierceness have caused many problems for Vietnam and Vietnam-U.S relations. My memory is limited to be able to list all problems that we faced during the preparation for the BTA.

- But surely there were there unforgettable problems?

- There was a perception that "the United States is basically a long-term enemy", along with anti-American and suspicious sentiment. Some people reckoned that the BTA was "a United States' plot to transform the Vietnamese political regime, simply (it) aimed to undermine the leadership of the Party".

Or using the free market to undermine the socialist orientation in our socialist-oriented market economy.

- *What did you think at that time?*

- There were consequences of a long process of separating from the market's rules and developing the monopolized socialist economy. These made us surprised and embarrassed when being forced to switch to the market economy and play by new rules which had been applied to most other countries.

Although the Party's Resolutions were repeatedly pointed out and the society has been aware that the world is changing profoundly and the global economy is flourishing and quickly following the globalization trend, it was not easy and quick to surmount the above-mentioned political and psychological barriers. Also, it was impossible for that to change overnight.

- *Could you please clarify in the BTA case?*

- Negotiating the BTA with the United States was completely new work. No one could imagine what it would be like. Every individual and agency had different perspectives and requests. No one was the same.

Now, it's fun to recall. Many issues raised appeared to challenge the negotiating delegations.

- *Challenging?*

- Because it was impossibly implemented.

For example, someone said: "In the past, we couldn't claim war reparations under the Paris Agreement (1973), we need to claim these in this negotiation".

We claimed reparations because we didn't understand U.S law. Money questions are decided by Congress, furthermore, Congress couldn't issue a Resolution on compensation as the United States thought it didn't lose in the war.

Of course, we had the right to claim compensation, but the United States wouldn't agree to include it in the negotiation.

Or, someone said that "The negotiating delegation has to fight with the United States to re-qualify Vietnam among the underdeveloped countries, so that they can offer Vietnam special preferential policies".

We found it unacceptable. Vietnam used to be named in the list of underdeveloped countries, like several African countries.

Vietnam felt our pride was hurt; it took the country many years to fight and mobilize to be listed among developing countrics. But, thc BTA negotiating delegation was then assigned to put Vietnam in a low ranking. What power did the U.S negotiating delegation have in ranking Vietnam up or down?

Others directed specifically: "The negotiation with the United States needs to implement the motto "both cooperating and fighting, and with a former foe like the United States, fighting is the main policy".

In my sense, it was no longer a war in which we won and the enemy lost. Both sides had to reach an agreement that ensured mutual benefits, thereby being long-term partners.

But, Joe Damond mentioned the story in the autumn of 1997 or so, during a negotiation, Nguyen Dinh Luong said that Vietnam was a poor and underdeveloped country, and would only possibly accept international trade standards (WTO) by 2020.

Please explain clearly.

- It was true. I now still find it funny when thinking about. This was because following my request, the U.S side prepared a "comprehensive" draft, based on WTO standards. Everyone was a bit shocked: "It's so confusing and new!"

May I interrupt you? Why did you request the partner to draw up a draft?

- At a meeting of the Vietnamese side, one person said that it was necessary for Nguyen Dinh Luong to provide a draft and state Vietnamese viewpoints with the United States.

Previously, when negotiating with the Soviet Union, it took me only three hours to complete a draft in both Russian and Vietnamese.

But attending the meeting of Ambassador Charlene Barshefsky and Minister of Trade Le Van Triet in Washington DC in June, 1995 and sat with Joe Damond until 12:00 a.m at the Sheraton Hotel to hear explanation on the concept of a comprehensive agreement under the commitments of the WTO, I realized I knew nothing about the WTO.

That was the reason why I required Damond to prepare the draft.

- *Yes. Please go on.*

- When we translated the draft, and submitted it to Vietnamese leaders for comments, someone said that Vietnam was a poor country and underdeveloped country, so, it would only possibly accept those standards by 2020.

Receiving those comments and the fact that our negotiating delegation hadn't prepared anything, we had to give the U.S side plans and roadmaps in all fields (trade, investment, services…) to be applied by 2020.

It was a shock to the U.S delegation. Looking at their faces, I knew they were very disappointed. They didn't expect...

- *Were they disappointed in people sitting opposite them?*

- Right. And since then, the story couldn't progress, as Joe Damond told you earlier.

But thanks to that, we could understand their real thoughts, and receive the strongest reactions, until then, from them. We needed to fully understand the U.S ideas in this game so that we could make plans. Hence, we had more time for studying and preparing.

Greater challenge outside the Vietnam-U.S negotiation

"Morever, he couldn't understand the fact that in Vietnam at that time, there was only one way of thinking: "Poverty was caused by the war. There was no way for anyone to say differently".

Huynh Phan (Vietnamnet - 2011)

- Joe Damond emphasized the second point, related to the Vietnam's proposal to entirely open up doors by 2020, that "Vietnam must consider the isolated market to be the cause of poverty and underdevelopment." How did you think at that time?

- Joe was completely right: In the world, countries that are open to international trade tend to grow faster without suffering poverty.

But he did not understand the specific circumstances in Vietnam. Going through 30 years of continuous wars, along with being politically surrounded by hostile countries and imposing an economic embargo, Vietnam found no way to open the door to the outside world.

Moreover, he didn't know our inner story. In fact, in Vietnam at that time, there was only one way thinking: Poverty was caused by the war. It was unacceptable to say differently.

But, truly thanks to Joe's frank remarks, we found it much easier to talk.

- Joe Damond said that it was not until the beginning of 1998 when he received the negotiation design from Vietnam that he believed the two sides could go on the same road before reaching a common goal.

During 8 months, how did you manage to complete the draft?

During that time, I met experienced people to learn from them.

First, I went to Saigon to meet people who had studied in the United States or worked for international organizations, including Professor Nguyen Xuan Oanh who worked for the IMF for two terms.

Nevertheless, they couldn't help me because in the 60s, they mainly studied GATT, not WTO.

I had to immediately travel abroad to seek help from my old friends. China was the first country that came to my mind, but, conversations didn't bring any results. So I arrived in Eastern Europe.

- Was it better, sir?

- I didn't obtain anything in Russia. In Poland, it was said that the BTA they signed with the United States was just a passport for them to join the EU and NATO, so they accepted all terms that the United States proposed.

Only when I arrived in Hungary did I see a glimmer of hope. My friend, who then was Assistant to the Hungarian Minister of Economy, told me:

"In my industry, there are many talented international negotiators, including in GATT. However, when returning to your home country, you must request that the Ministry of Trade to send me an official letter to ask for a grant of several hundred thousand U.S dollars. With that amount of money, I will send experts to assist you".

I was glad to return. While rushing to ask for signatures and seals, I heard the news that the ruling Democratic Party was overthrown and the Youth Party took over.

- How bad your fate was. What happened then?

- At that time, the Government allowed us to invite the U.S consultants. And Ginny Foote showed up.

The U.S-Vietnam Trade Council invited professors and experts to lecture on WTO for the negotiating delegation. After listening to pilot lectures at different classes, I chose Dan Price.

- Why?

- He was then working for a consulting firm in the United States. But Dan had worked for the U.S Trade Representative for a long time and most importantly, he negotiated the BTA with the Soviet Union and NAFTA (North American Free Trade Agreement). I thought he could provide us with what we needed.

- Joe Damond said that Dan Price played a certain role in helping Vietnam to complete an adjusted negotiation design, didn't he?

- Dan Price was a good, experienced and knowledgeable consultant. When he became Deputy National Security Adviser in charge of economic foreign affairs in the Bush administration (son), we remained friends. Whenever he arrived in Hanoi, he invited me for a few drinks.

Returning to the story in 1997, when there were issues that needed to be considered, I always asked Dan to put forward 4-5 plans, or at least 2.

Opting for which solutions or whether to adjust or not was decided by the Vietnamese negotiation delegation. Because we had to recommended the most suitable plan based on conditions in Vietnam.

During that time, I assigned everyone to learn and redesign each area, from intellectual property, investment to services. Professional experts reviewed what needed to be removed, changed, or added in the U.S plan. Lawyers worked together every week to analyze each concept, sentence and paragraph...to find better, more simple words, we guaranteed that we would definitely not commit unless we fully understood the contents.

The final design was much changed compared to one of the United States proposed 8 months ago. In particular, the Chapter of Trade in Services was entirely rewritten to suit the conditions of Vietnam.

And as Joe said, since May 1988, the negotiation had become essential, and we only focused on discussing roadmaps to open the market.

Well, Joe Damond said that Dan Price only informed him that Vietnam's design would be much changed but didn't specify how it would be changed.

He added another point which surprised you which was how Luong could persuade the Government and relevant agencies of Vietnam to agree with that design.

Please explain this clearly.

- When preparation was completed, we submitted to seniority a 350-page report, each person received one.

Did you face any difficulty with your report?

- Yes, nothing was easy. People objected because in all investment agreements which Vietnam had signed with other countries, content like this had never been seen.

A colleague in the Trade Ministry told me that the negotiators' responsibility was to draw up the report so that the legal framework wouldn't collide with the existing legal framework.

I had to say that our legal framework had so many limitations that it needed to be revised in order to take effect.

We convinced opponents with the argument that: Countries could hardly develop without exporting to the US market.

Even China could not successfully implement its "Four Modernizations" unless it signed the BTA with the United States to enjoy most-favored-nation (MFN) status to boost exports.

If Vietnam wanted to export, the country needed to develop a legal system to meet that demand. And for long-term development, it shouldn't just be changed in small ways.

There were firm objections in the Intellectual Property Chapter. The criticism that capitalist countries could develop because they "stole" others' inventions, and if Vietnam committed to join it meant "tying our hands", and it wouldn't be affordable to buy products later.

We had to persuade them that there would not be any investors from the United States and other developed countries feeling insecure to invest in Vietnam without a commitment for their products to not be counterfeited.

Moreover, the United States considers intellectual property as being in the national interest and giving enterprise benefits. There was no way they would give that up.

For instance, just the brand value of Coca-Cola ($90 billion) was nearly three times Vietnam's GDP at that time ($32 bil).

Or in the Investment Chapter, we also had to persuade them that our target was attracting investment, hence, it was essential to improve the regulatory environment.

Or in the Government Procurement Chapter, many people strongly opposed the regulation requiring state investment projects of half a million USD or more to be bid. They argued that bidding would reveal national secrets.

We responded that only civilian projects of building power plants or purchasing trains would be bid and ones related to security and defense were exempted.

We asserted that instead of awarding bids, publicly tendering was the only way to restrict corruption.

But this chapter was finally removed.

- *Was that your greatest pain?*

- For the agreement, it was true that it was the greatest pain. But with the Vietnamese negotiating delegation and I, the biggest pain laid elsewhere. I will say later.

The sorrow of the BTA negotiator

"I had a hunch that something wasn't well, when senior leaders had a meeting again to discuss for the last time about signing the BTA. However, I still believed that everything would be OK".

Huynh Phan (Vietnamnet-December 29, 2011)

- As you know, the great Russian writer Lev Tolstoy said that the agreement would only be reached if one of two people understood the other's true intentions. In the case of the BTA, it took the two sides one year and a half, with five rounds of negotiations to do so.

However, the difference for the BTA, was that both Vietnam and the United States understood each other's real intentions to move forward.

Only from the sixth round of negotiation, did you realize changes in the United States' attitude towards you and the Vietnamese negotiation delegation?

Yes, it was very clear. Through their attitude, eyes and words. Earlier, I realized their anxiety.

In addition, as Joe told you, it would be surely hard to negotiate with a person who was trained in the Soviet Union and had worked with the Soviet Union and Eastern Europe according to the Soviet commercial model for many years.

Once we understood each other, Joe told me that he had waited for the worst to happen.

- I would like to ask you again. Joe Damond said that the U.S chief was the "boss" of the games but the Vietnamese chief acted as a coordinator of negotiations. Was there any reason, or it was your personality?

- Normally, in negotiations, especially at the beginning, I asked many questions and also required people in the delegation to raise questions.

First, the more information we got, the more we understood the partner's intentions. On the other hand, we would also have the chance to learn more about the market economy so that we could better protect Vietnam's real interests.

The same as Joe Damond and the US negotiation delegation in protecting US national interests.

Second, the Vietnamese negotiating team was an inter-ministerial delegation, each ministry had its own interests, each with its own agenda. If the delegation leader did not know how to coordinate well, it was easy to happen that "the team leader may have created a confused and controversial negotiation plan among ministries".

For instance, I asked Tuan (Ha Huy Tuan, who later was the Vice President of the National Financial Supervision Commission) to prepare for tariff negotiations, then submit it to Nguyen Sinh Hung (Minister of Finance that time) for signing before addressing the the Prime Minister.

On investment, I asked An (Dinh Van An, who later was the General Secretary's Assistant), to prepare, then submit to the Deputy Minister Vo Hong Phuc to initial.

Regarding intellectual property, I asked Chien (Do Khac Chien - Former Deputy Director General of the Copyright Office - Ministry of Culture and Information) and Chuong (Pham Dinh Chuong - Former Director General of Intellectual Property Office - Ministry of Science, Technology and Environment) to prepare a draft and submit to the ministers for initialing.

Of course I had discussed in detail and reached consensus with Tuan, An, Chien and Truong in advance on how to implement the plan. After having all ministers' signatures, they sent me a copy to summarize into a joint proposal, which was then submitted to our superiors to be passed.

Though I was the chief negotiator and the one who took all responsibility if any problem arose, I still had to respect my comrades, respect their knowledge and contribution, especially their rights.

Today, things like promoting or attracting all social resources and social intelligence is often mentioned too; however, how can we attract or promote what we haven't attached much importance to.

- *Wasn't it ironic that Joe Damond, a man coming from the so-called land of freedom, behaved like a dictator, as he admitted when talking to me, while the working style of Vietnam's representatives was...*

- (Laughing) The U.S. side was different. The USTR was formed to negotiate trade agreements, as well as to deal with international trade disputes. They are so professional.

- Back to the negotiation, from the 6th talks until both sides' initialing, which took place more than a year later, did everything go smoothly?

- When negotiating on tax, I asked Joe Damond to compile U.S. requirements for me. And when we sat around the negotiation table, they gave me a very long list on a tariff reduction framework, and did not forget to emphasize that their Congress would not approve otherwise.

In the Congress, congressmen are backed by enterprises. And, they would not support unless enterprises gained interests in the deal.

- Oh, Joe Damond did tell this story, and said that at first he was so surprised at your proposal...

- When discussing on the basis of that list, I told Joe that import taxes (i.e., tariffs) only accounted for 2% of the US revenue, mainly supporting trade policy purpose, while in Vietnam, it accounted for 20% of the revenue.

If income from export had not much improved yet while we suddenly lost 1/5 of our revenue after signing the BTA, of course Vietnam's government would not agree.

I also further explained that the United States had personal income tax, property tax amongst others, while in Vietnam at that time, people's income was not enough to pay for their meals, and most people had little property. I myself was living in a state-owned house. What did we have to make up for that deficit!

Then I said: "Well, we will discuss this, but later, when Vietnam negotiates to join the WTO. Until then, Vietnam also has several years to reform its tax system to suit the world, such as VAT, income tax, property tax etc."

Joe got my point, the two sides discussed back and forth, then finally we only focused on more than 200 kinds of tariffs to discuss tariff rates and tariff reduction schedule.

But problems were not yet solved. When the two sides' tariff groups entered their negotiation, the United States again asked Vietnam to show the AFTA tariff rate (ASEAN Free Trade Area). Tuan and Khanh (currently Deputy Minister of Industry and Trade, TPP Chief Negotiator), did not agree and reported to me.

That evening, Joe invited us for dinner.

During the meal, I asked: "Does the US side have any intention to sign the BTA?" Joe looked at me surprisingly. I continued: "Why does your tariff group make such a request? The US side wants our AFTA tariff rate, then in return, please show us the NAFTA tariff rate (North American Free Trade Agreement). Only then can we discuss".

Joe gave in, and things got much easier. If you [journalist] would like to learn more about negotiation details, you should ask Tuan or Khanh.

- When Joe Damond informed you in Auckland that the BTA signing was delayed, is it true that you knew nothing in advance?

- I did have a feeling that something was not going well when high-level leaders met again to discuss BTA signing for the last time. Because total consensus was already reached before. But I still believed that everything would be alright. Therefore, upon being informed by Joe, I was greatly surprised. I nearly could not believe it to be so.

- Did you buy into Joe's explanation?

- There was a time when sitting with Ginny Foote, referring to that missed boat, I said tongue in cheek "women are great at solving things, yet sometimes they are also great at messing things up". Everyone burst out laughing.

- Yeah, Ms. Albright, when serving as the US Ambassador to the United Nations, once threatened to break Secretary-General Boutros Boutros – Ghali's legs.

What was your feeling when you better understood the failure's reasons?

- Sad, deeply sad, for many reasons. Afterwards, there were issues that we had to explain over and over again.

- When did high-level leaders agree to resume negotiation to sign the BTA?

- After explanation, we received no comment. In December 1999, we again made a report asking to sign [the BTA].

Early 2000, the Ministry of Trade had a change in its leadership. Vu Khoan, Permanent Deputy Minister of Foreign Affairs, replaced Truong Dinh Tuyen, who was sent to Nghe An province

Right after being appointed, Vu Khoan came to see me and said: "We old friends must complete the BTA for our satisfied retirement." We both studied in MGIMO (Moscow State Institute of International Relations), though not in the same year.

After Tet, in the middle of March, I sent Joe and the US delegation an invitation to visit Vietnam. Joe would have liked to, but both the Department of State and the USTR were cautious of Vietnam after the postponement in Auckland.

- Did Joe mention Dan Price's role in this?

- Yes, he did. We invited Dan to visit. Everything became clear to the US side.

However in July 2000, they still challenged us for the last time, by inviting Minister Vu Khoan to the US. If Vu Khoan agreed, it would mean that both parties were determined to sign the deal.

- What do you remember most from that last negotiation?

Joe and I only needed half an hour to solve everything, leaving three provisions that needed solving at ministerial level.

In addition to the memory that is still kept on the wall, which is a photo capturing President Bill Clinton shaking my hand, there is a warm memory when Minister Vu Khoan insisted on waiting for "Mr. Luong" to finish the work before getting in the car together to go to the White House. Haha, the two old friends…

- Joe Damond has written a memoir, which is expected to be published next year. How about you?

My friends also advised and urged me to write one. I will consider it.

Looking back 10 years to the implementing of the Vietnam – U.S. BTA, Nguyen Dinh Luong said that he was less pleased to see significant rise in exports than to find the BTA's legal weight helping Vietnam break its subsidized economy's "stagnation iceberg", pull down poles supporting the ineffective "beg-give" economy, break the lock to allow "WTO wind" to blow into every meeting room, ballroom, lecture hall, library, and dismantle the legal box made of material named "monopoly" and "discrimination"...

And then designing a new legal framework in line with international standards while removing obstacles in the process of implementing Party and State's policy, which was activating all social potential for development.

In my period, no one believed in Vietnam-US friendship

"Near the Ministry of Trade (today the Ministry of Industry and Trade) on Trang Tien street, a US expert team came across an illegal counterfeit of Microsoft disks sold at 5,000 Vietnam dong [equal to 2 pence], while the authentic one was 50 U.S. dollars. How could they not get mad!".

Phuong Anh (Vn Express – July 11, 2020)

On July 13, 2000, at a press conference in the White House, only a few minutes after the U.S-Vietnam Bilateral Trade Agreement (BTA) was signed, U.S. President Bill Clinton thanked three Vietnamese who contributed to the process leading to the Agreement. They were Vu Khoan – Minister of Trade, Nguyen Dinh Luong – BTA Chief Negotiator and Le Van Bang – Vietnamese Ambassador.

20 years later, still with the sonorous voice of a negotiator, Nguyen Dinh Luong said to VnExpress: "At that time I said to myself that even if I died on the negotiating table, I would do it at all costs. The whole world needs the United States to develop, and Vietnam could not stand out. The stubborn willpower will be pushed out by the wheels of history."

- What was the context when you were assigned [to negotiate] this trade agreement?

- When receiving the mission, I already had nearly 20 years working in the field, but I mostly negotiated with socialist countries. They had comradeship, the same institution, and the same legal system as Vietnam. But the BTA was completely different.

When the Soviet Union dissolved, I went to negotiate with countries such as Singapore, Switzerland, Norway, Canada. But they were not the United States. Back then I understood nothing about the US, I only knew that they were difficult to negotiate with. Even the European, Japanese, and Chinese were struggled when negotiating with the US.

At that time, the leaders already determined that the negotiation's goal was to normalize economic and trade relations, to complete the relations normalizing process with the US. Vietnam had already normalized diplomatic relations before.

However, when negotiating, we understood that we needed two additional goals. The first was to get Vietnam to join the WTO, from which the country could integrate into the world. The BTA would be the foundation and the necessary condition.

The second was to build a long-term business partnership with the USA, which was a very important goal. This goal needed to be achieved through a suitable negotiation plan which could build mutual trust. Thanks to that method and also through frank and honest communication, the delegation had created good relations with U.S. negotiators. Once we trusted each other, everything would be simpler. In the end, after the five-year-long marathon, all three goals were thoroughly reached.

- So what did you do to understand the Americans before entering the negotiation?

- I read, which took me the greatest amount of time in the 5 years of negotiating. I looked for books written about the USA, from history, culture, politics, law to development advantages.

From those books, I became aware of the U.S. economic power. I realized how they were manipulating international economic organizations. You must understand the Americans to sit and talk with them.

I also studied agreements that the US had signed with other nations, regulatory documents of economic and trade organizations such as GATT, WTO. If you do not understand the WTO's rules, you won't be able to negotiate with the Americans.

- *What do you think was the biggest difficulty when negotiating the BTA with the US?*

- It was trust. The legacy of the Vietnam war was too serious and painful. When referring to the Americans, the society thought of war, bombs, bullets and death. For both leaders and citizens, it was difficult to accept the Americans' return and they were still worried that the US had a scheme to destroy Vietnam. On the other hand, due to failure in the war, the Americans also doubted Vietnam's good will.

In September 1999, the BTA was supposed to be signed in Auckland, New Zealand, however, it failed because the two countries lacked trust in each other. After that, negotiators struggled to find ways to build social consensus, to have a common vision for the future.

In addition, we faced several other difficulties such as the Vietnamese' lack of information. Newspapers at that time did not write about the United States. And the negotiation's context was highly unfavorable.

Vietnam negotiated the BTA in the time of globalization. However, some theorists in the country believed that globalization was a capitalist game which only brought poverty and widened the income gap. Therefore, Vietnam did not have access to the rapid changes in the global economy. The WTO was founded in 1995, while I was negotiating the BTA, yet hardly any news about this organization appeared in the country.

The domestic economy at that time was subsidized, planned, and dominated. There were very small things such as electricity price, water price, airplane tickets, train tickets, and tourism tickets that had up to 2 prices, discriminating between citizens and foreigners.

The BTA's value was to push Vietnam to drop its subsidized economy, which was clearly out of date. The BTA forced Vietnam's economy to take a different track, to play by international rules.

- So when the Agreement came into force, what problems did Vietnam face?

- Once we made commitments, we had to comply with them. Vietnam had to amend the law to better suit [the BTA]. To do this, the government assigned the Ministry of Justice to host and coordinate with other ministries and agencies to review the entire legal system and compare it with the BTA's commitments. Based on that, we built a law-making program to submit to the National Assembly. We had to find which laws needed amending and supplementing.

I remember that the Trade Law was published in 1995, but in 2000 when we finished negotiating the BTA, none of its provisions came into practice.

The Intellectual Property Chapter had up to 80 articles, but near the Ministry of Trade (nowadays the Ministry of Industry and Trade) on Trang Tien street, the US expert team came across an illegal counterfeit of a Microsoft disk sold at 5,000 dong, while the authentic one was 50 U.S. dollars. How could they not get mad! But we could not handle that because the law had no enforcement provisions, no one was assigned to deal with violations.

After reviewing, I remember that we had to amend and supplement 173 regulations. The National Assembly in the following term had to continuously make and amend the law!

- Today when looking back at the BTA after 20 years, what did you regret the most in the negotiation that could have given Vietnam more benefits?

- I am actually satisfied with what we achieved. When we went to the negotiation, not many people understood what the BTA was. It had disadvantages but also advantages because we achieved our goal to break the conservativeness, for Vietnam's rules of game to get close to that of the world.

In the negotiation reports, we only focused on explaining the BTA's benefits and the necessity to establish trade relations with the US.

As for the commitments and the fact that we had to change and remove something here and there, after the Agreement came into effect, they had to effectively be handled.

There were of course "conspiracies" that failed. For example, in the Government Procurement Agreement; we felt really unpleased about the method to appoint contractors, which was neither open nor transparent. We found ways to "sneak through" so that projects must be publicly bid, but in the end, we still got caught, so we lost! (Laughing loud).

- What do you imagine could have happened if the BTA could not have been negotiated at that time?

- The Vietnam-U.S. Bilateral Trade Agreement came into effect in December 2001. All goods exported from Vietnam to the US were entitled to the most-favored-nation tariff, also known as unconditional normal trade relations. Its basic principle is that when the two countries grant the best treatment to a third country, they must also grant each other the same thing.

The BTA negotiation was extremely difficult but I think that it had to be done. The whole world rushed into the U.S market to develop. Take China, Japan, Korea as examples. So, why would we stand outside?

I did not think that the negotiation would fail. We needed to do it at all costs. Even if we died on the negotiating table, the Agreement had to be signed!

- As one of the people who contributed to promoting the Vietnam – US relations, what do you think about the relations

between the two countries, especially in the field of economy, after 25 years?

- In the past 25 years, from adversaries, the United States and Vietnam have become friends and partners. In this development process, the economy is the pillar. The faster the economy develops, the more exchanges the two countries have, and the better understanding and trust are built and reinforced.

Currently, Vietnam and the US have trust in each other, from which cooperation in other fields, such as security and defense, can be developed.

In addition, geopolitical factors should also be taken into account. Vietnam's position is very important in the eyes of the Americans. The US cannot deploy whatever strategy in Asia-Pacific without Vietnam's support.

- How are economic achievements in the two countries' relations now compared to what you initially wanted 25 years ago?

- The current outcome is something I did not dare to think of at the time of the negotiation. No one would have thought that the import and export turnover of the two countries today could reach nearly 80 billion U.S. dollars, compared to $ 450 million in 1995. Also, no one dared imagine that the US and Vietnam could establish comprehensive partnership relations.

- When celebrating the BTA's 10th anniversary, you said that U.S. FDI into Vietnam did not meet expectations. 10 years later, many experts still referred to it. What do you think the reason is?

- The first reason is that Vietnam lies next to a too attractive 1,4-billion-people market. Almost all major US economic groups have focused on exploiting China's market. This is an objective factor. For investors, this benefit is most important.

Another reason is that Vietnam's legal and trade environment is not "clean" enough despite the country's efforts to improve. The laws are overlapping, the procedures and administration works are still troublesome, corruption still widely exists.

American corporations do business in a professional way, and they do not like "cheating". To enter a market, they have to research and build long-term strategies. They will only invest when they are surely confident with the money spent.

- *How do you evaluate opportunities to attract FDI investment from the US, especially recently when the Covid-19 pandemic is fueling production shift?*

- American businesses will calculate the benefits of leaving China at Trump's call and the benefits of staying to see which one will prevail in both short and long terms.

If they have to move their factories, they will carefully study the destinations to ensure that their money will continue to gain benefits. They will consider it very carefully. In general, they will follow the direction of benefits, not of the President or anyone else. Therefore, I think there will not be a "flow of pure gold decorated with American star flag" immediately pouring into Vietnam as some people have anticipated.

Besides, I see some sources saying that the US will join Vietnam in restructuring the global supply chain. However, it is just an idea, not yet a policy. I haven't seen anything specific yet.

In the future, if that idea comes true, Vietnam will have the final say. Do we have a legal and business environment that is good and transparent enough for them to want to invest in?

- Under the Donald Trump administration, the United States seemed to reduce multilateral cooperation and prioritize bilateral relations. How do you think future economic cooperation with the US should be, especially when relations between countries are becoming increasingly multi-dimensional and complex?

- American politicians have different stances on globalization from time to time. The Presidents Bill Clinton and Barack Obama administrations both encouraged globalization and stimulated American economic groups to exploit the openness and resources of the world economy. This strategy has brought great benefits to the US economy in the long run.

Under President Trump's administration, he thinks that the period when the US has to subsidize the world is over, US corporations must stop going out, benefiting other countries. In Trump's opinion, Americans are first.

He does not completely rule out globalization but his policies are protectionist. However, the U.S. economy also cannot be separated from the global economy. Therefore, Trump wanted to rewrite the rules of the game.

Trump cannot immediately amend the rules formed in international economic organizations. Instead, he step by step amends the rules of each block, such as NAFTA, Korea, Japan, and soon the UK and EU.

Once he can amend the rules in bilateral relations, President Trump will think of reforming the WTO to ensure the organization's balance of benefits and effectiveness.

Vietnam's current biggest problem with the US is trade deficit, which was about 40 billion U.S. dollars in 2019. The United States has raised this issue to us, but not too harsh. Besides, Vietnam has approached and shown interest in improving the situation. The two sides have established mechanisms to handle and jointly review blockages in trade relations.

Vietnam also actively buys more US goods, from agricultural products to aircraft. Actually I think there is a better way, which is that we improve the business environment to attract more investment from US. This will help the two countries' economic and trade relations become more balanced and sustainable.

Story about the White House's "gift" or bittersweet memories of a photo

"As soon as they met, the American friends told me: "Luong, you have a special gift." He was so surprised that he asked them over and over again what the gift was, who gave it to him. American friends always had close feelings for Luong, but they insisted on keeping the secret."

Xuan Phuong (Vietnam Economic News – Spring 2016)

15 years after coming into effect, the Vietnam-US Bilateral Trade Agreement not only helped Vietnam - US trade develop spectacularly, but it also opened up a positive future for the Vietnamese economy to access a series of new opportunities, integrating into the global economy, as well as joining the WTO, and negotiating a new generation of FTAs.

In the mind of Nguyen Dinh Luong – Vietnam's Chief Negotiator, memories of the 5-year "marathon race" to sign the BTA, with all its struggles and bittersweetness, is still as fresh as if it had taken place just yesterday.

The BTA "fight", a long journey with many memories and problems with the other side, and also this side, lasted for 5 years. Among those memories, the Chief Negotiator remembers special photo for a life time.

He cannot forget the photo because it is attached to both sweet joy and bitter sadness.

He said: on the afternoon of July 13, 2020, the BTA was signed. Vietnam's Minister of Trade and Chief Negotiator were invited to the White House to meet the U.S. President.

The first and surely the only time Luong was invited to the White House to meet the U.S. President, he put a camera into his pocket, hoping to capture some photos of this historic meeting. However, when arrived at the White House, he was asked not to take photos. Taking photos of the president in the White House was the job of White House reporters and theirs only.

More than a year later, in November 2001, President Bill Clinton visited Hanoi, Luong got a chance to reunite with his friends from the America. As soon as they met, the American friends told him: "Luong, you have a special gift." He was so surprised that he asked them over and over again what the gift was, who gave it to him. American friends always had close feelings for Luong, but they insisted on keeping the secret. What was the gift? Who gave him this gift? He thought about those questions all night but still had no idea.

Around 11:00 am the day after, the secret about that gift was revealed as American friends gave Luong a beautiful photo frame brought from the US, with a photo capturing the moment when Luong was received and shook hands with President Bill Clinton in the White House. He was very surprised, happy and emotional.

The American friends also repeatedly said: this was a special gift because not everyone who entered the White House could take photos with the President and not everyone taken in photos with the President was given the photos.

The natural and intimate moment when Vietnam Chief Negotiator shook hands with the US President was fully captured. The straight postures, the bright smiles, the two looking straight into each other's eyes with a respectful attitude, shaking hands.

Today, with the same clever eyes, the same kind smile, the Chief Negotiator said: "This photo was taken in the Roosevelt room by the White House. To me, this is the most valuable gift in my life, also a thing that rarely happens in the life of a negotiator like me."

He explained, he was so fond of the photo because he liked and respected Clinton very much. To him, Clinton is an idol for many reasons. He considers this photo a special gift, a reward, an appreciation, a recognition. Several minutes before taking the photo, in a speech at a press conference, which was held in the Rose Garden next to the living room and broadcast live by CNN, Clinton thanked everyone who had been involved and contributed to the BTA negotiating process. Among them, Clinton thanked Vietnamese Chief Negotiator Nguyen Dinh Luong.

Luong said that in order to negotiate with the US, he had to learn and know by heart the rules of the game, he had to read and understand the Americans. He also searched for information about the president-in-office.

Not only having a handsome, elegant, polite, intelligent appearance, Clinton is also the person who, in his position as the United States president, quickly removed legal obstacles to open a new page in the US-Vietnam relations.

When he was younger, at the age to register for military service, Clinton avoided involvement in the Vietnam War by going to London, England, to join a university course. When he entered the White House, he soon removed from his mind the heavy thoughts about the past war to normalize relations with Vietnam, closing pages of painful history between the two peoples.

Luong continued: on June 30, 2000, the Vietnam negotiation delegation landed in Washington D.C. The remaining issues in the negotiation also were completed quickly. Luong and Joseph Damond, US Chief Negotiator discussed and agreed to report to both sides' ministers so that they would meet to finish the negotiation and sign the Agreement on July 11, 2000.

But, Joseph Damond informed Luong that the signing time and date would be decided by the White House, and depended on the President's working agenda. The President wanted to have the right to be the first to announce Vietnam-US BTA signing. At that time, President Bill Clinton was "struggling" with the negotiation between Israel and Palestine in David Camp (a U.S. navy base – Reporter), so [the BTA signing] had to wait. And it did not have to wait too long. President Clinton gave the negotiation in David Camp a few hour "break", got on a helicopter, returning to the White House.

It was at 4 pm on July 13, 2000 that the historic press release about an important event of the United States and Vietnam began. The event was broadcasted live by CNN, reported by hundreds of American reporters and watched by the whole world. Clinton emotionally delivered his speech:

"...Just a few moments ago, Ambassador Barshefsky and Minister Vu Khoan signed the agreement between the United States and Vietnam... And so, from the bitter past, we plant the seeds of a better future...This agreement is one more reminder that the former adversaries can come together to find a common ground in a way of benefits for the peoples, to let go over the past and embrace the future, to forgive and to reconcile".

Luong added that sometimes when he looked at the photo, he felt like tasting bitterness and sting in the tongue, that was when he recalled the "fights". He said that once in a meeting, he suggested that we should have signed the BTA under President Clinton administration, because in the history of Vietnam – US relations, no US president had treated Vietnam better than President Clinton. He tried to close painful pages in the relations to rewrite new ones. Then, someone told Luong that he had "delusive stance about class. As an imperialist leader, he must have been not good to Vietnam." Luong was deeply sad. But then, he understood that it was how things went at that time. The wounds of the war were still painful, the gap between the US and Vietnam was still very wide. The US was still a dangerous foe.

However, Luong also would like to tell that people who were responsible to join this new journey, including himself, that they must first overcome themselves to seek benefits for the nation when great changes were made at the time. If we keep holding on to the hatred of the past, the nation would not be able hold its head up high.

Three peak joys of the negotiator

"After two days, Peterson convinced the US Congress that:"
Vietnam is a unique nation. To Vietnam, we can only
persevere with but not force".

Hoang Hai Van (Thanh nien - 2002)

"My father taught me, as a plowman, that the plow path must be straight. If you want to have a straight line, you must pay attention: When you are plowing, your eyes need to see far away, hold the plow, let your hand relax to be flexible, but when the plow crosses the hard ground, the hand must be tight. Today, I always remember what my father taught when working as a negotiator," said Nguyen Dinh Luong, Chief negotiator of Vietnamese negotiating delegation for the Vietnam-US Trade Agreement.

The man said he, together with Vietnamese Trade Minister Le Van Triet, arrived in Washington DC on May 20, 1996. The US handed over a document on negotiation principles to the Vietnamese side. They said, as Vietnam had registered to join the World Trade Organization (WTO), it was a must to base on WTO rules to negotiate a comprehensive agreement, covering trade in goods and services, intellectual property, investment and so on. US Trade Representative Charlene Barshefsky said coldly (contrary to her enthusiasm later): "The problem lies with Vietnam's building of a socialist-oriented economy." Le Van Triet, in reply, said this would not be a hurdle as Vietnam had affirmed its willingness to cooperate with countries with different social and political regimes.

During a talk with Joe Damond (later the US chief negotiator) in a bar in the Sheraton hotel from 7pm to 12pm that day, Luong learned about the US side's intentions and views. "At that time, I knew what I should do," he said. After the meeting, he outlined five principles of negotiation. When the Trade Ministry submitted the principles to the Government, Prime Minister Vo Van Kiet wrote "agree" on the pages. The next day, the ministry received a response document, saying "agree with the Trade Ministry's proposals." Understanding views and intentions of the US to prepare for the competition of brainpower was the first joy.

The second joy, he continued, came at the opening ceremony of the fifth negotiation round, also held in Washington DC in May 1998. Unlike the previous rounds, he met new negotiators: the US Ambassador to WTO, the US Vice Trade Representative who was also head of the US negotiation delegation for services and the US Intellectual Property Representative in Geneva, head of the US negotiation delegation for investment, among others. US Ambassador to Vietnam, Peterson, was also present at the meeting. "What is happening," he asked himself. He said the US gave Vietnam in April 1997 a draft agreement that had been drawn up on the basis of WTO rules. "The US were serious when mentioning WTO rules." The draft was also forwarded to a number of other countries that signed right in the year. The Vietnamese side, however, had not inked immediately as it found that commitments would be unfavorable towards the country. Therefore, Vietnam suggested re-outlining the agreement, making it match the country's situation, explaining "Vietnam is still a developing country." Before the trip, Vietnam had sent another draft agreement to the US, which was different from that compiled by the country. The US side was so astonished that Vietnam refused to sign their document, while other countries had reached it. After consulting experts, the US finally agreed with the document sketched out by Vietnam. Moreover, the US thanked Vietnam for putting forth a roadmap that would be applicable to countries with similar conditions, and had never been rolled out earlier.

US chief negotiator Joe Damond, in his opening remarks, said "We are very surprised and can say frankly that we are excited when having partners like you." Everyone knows that it is hard to negotiate with the US. Japan, Europe and China also shared the view. Luong said: "At that time, I felt joyful and swelled with national pride." Two days later, Peterson addressed a meeting of the US Congress that Vietnam was a unique nation, and they should only maintain persistence with Vietnam instead of force. He emphasized that it was a game of intelligence, and it must be won by intelligence. The draft, of course, was not the final, but both sides had seen the light. Each of them then took further steps backwards to reach the agreement.

The third joy was a life-long memorable experience. In the negotiating room on July 3, 2000, apart from US negotiators, there were four others from the US Department of State, which demonstrated the country's great attention to this round of talks. Luong told the person sitting next to him: "This is done." He referred to the US's intention to end the negotiation round to prepare for the Hanoi visit by Bill Clinton. Clinton wanted to write his name in history as a person who opened up a new page for the relations between Vietnam and the US (the normalization of the bilateral diplomatic ties). Therefore, the agreement must be inked during this round. Five days later, Trade Minister Vu Khoan, on behalf of the Vietnamese Government, and trade representative Barshefsky, on behalf of the US Government, officially signed the bilateral trade agreement at 2pm on July 13, 2000.

"Following the signing, I returned to the Vietnamese Trade Office in Washington, with a feeling of serenity." "I suddenly wanted something, but I didn't know exactly what it was. I spotted a bottle of Smirnoff on the bookshelf. It was great. I had not taken any sip of wine for a long time." Then, he told about his youth in retrospect when he was a true plowman and drank a lot. "I used to drink local rice wine in Vietnam and then Vodka in Russia. However, I have stopped that habit since working with Americans." Luong said he spent three consecutive weeks in San Francisco with parties during his first visit to the US in the summer of 1994. The parties, however, were alcohol free. In another banquet for the delegation of the US Department of Agriculture, hosted by Nguyen Cong Tan in Hanoi, none of the American guests had beer or wine although the alcohol was available. He then knew that most of Americans have kept the habit of no drinking at parties as most of them drive when going out. Meanwhile, drunk drivers would face stiff penalties. He decided to follow such good habit. "We should learn from their good practices ," he said.

Nghe An-born "plowman" in the "US-Vietnam trade field"

"Joe and I gradually understood each other. We often stared at each other with the same thought: trying to find common ground among multiple differences between us."

(Lo Giang – Investment Review – Special Issue July/2005)

Americans called him respectfully "Mr. Luong", while he called himself a "Nghe An-born plowman." The man who was on the short side, with a round face and smiling eyes while talking to others, with knowledge and a sense of humor is Nguyen Dinh Luong, Vietnam's chief negotiator for the US-Vietnam Bilateral Trade Agreement (BTA).

The BTA may be among the bilateral trade deals that underwent the longest negotiation period in the world, with five years and 11 rounds of talks. It is understandable as the Vietnam-US relationship is "so special", as Nguyen Dinh Luong said. "An unforgettable war in history, a present full of guilt and a future full of fears."

One year after the normalization of the bilateral diplomatic ties, the two "former foes" began the negotiations with a big gap, which, negotiators presumed, "would not be bridged" due to not only the burden left over from the past but also the big differences between the two sides. The US side had little idea of Vietnam's trade system, regulations and procedures." Meanwhile, the US trade system, rules and standards were almost as strange to Vietnam. It remained a great challenge for the Southeast Asian nation to engage in negotiations with the US, considered the most "hard-to-deal" partner, on the basis of WTO rules in the mid-1990s.

After five years of struggling in talks, many times it seemed that there would be no hope for the agreement until it was reached on July 13, 2020, marking the completion of the normalization of the bilateral diplomatic ties.

Joe Damond, the US former chief negotiator for the BTA, mentioned one of the reasons behind the success of the negotiations: "I really admire my partner – Nguyen Dinh Luong and his entourage. I have gradually understood their vision and have confidence in the man. I believe that he also understands and trusts me. Although we have different viewpoints and stances, both have tried to reach mutual understanding."

Meanwhile, "Mr. Luong" talked about his "vision" through a fatherhood story: "My father said as a plowman, I should create straight furrows by looking ahead while plowing, instead of locking eyes on the ox." During the negotiations with the US, Luong and his entourage had taken into consideration the era, Vietnam's future, and the current and future global situation.

During the five years of negotiations with many tough rounds, he sometimes felt exhausted right at the negotiating table. He then reminded himself: "The agreement benefits Vietnam. Americans never give anything freely. You may lose if you are not excellent when engaging in business with the US. Through the deal, Vietnam would catch up with other countries and escape from backwardness." Sharing Luong's hardships, Joe Damond cabled a congratulatory message to

Luong after learning about the Vietnamese National Assembly's ratification of the pact, saying "people will consider you a hero."

Friendship nurtured over five-years of negotiations

After years of talks, the Vietnamese and US chief negotiators have become close friends, as Luong said "Each time when we met, we had a heart-to-heart talk about all topics: our life, families and careers. We regularly exchanged information and missed each other."

"Joe and I used to be strangers who shared nothing in common. Moreover, we are of different generations. Joe grew up after the American war in Vietnam, so he had no insight into the war. Meanwhile, I grew up in the war and had to overcome myself, for the sake of the nation," Luong said.

What did turn the strangers, partners and rivals at the negotiating table into friends? Luong said their mutual respect and trust were formed when they were working together to seek solutions to their differences in a candid and honest manner.

"Trade talks are to build up a long-term partnership. The partnership requires mutual trust. The mutual trust must be based on candidness and honesty. I followed that motto during the talks with the US side. We frankly shared our difficulties to seek solutions together. Vietnam did not satisfy the US side's unreasonable demands. We made commitments in accordance with our capacity."

"Joe and I gradually understood each other. We often stared at each other with the same thought: trying to find common ground among multiple differences between us, and to fill our gap."

Joe, in his book on the BTA, reminisced on his first meeting with Nguyen Dinh Luong in September 1996 who then became Vietnam's main character in his story. Joe said he knew that Luong could speak Russian fluently as the Vietnamese man spent many years in Moscow. But Luong was not good at English. Joe was afraid that the worst would happen.

However, Joe admitted, his worries were baseless. Although Luong had not much knowledge about international trade standards initially, the Vietnamese chief negotiator surprised Joe with his sharp mind. Moreover, Luong was a charming man and was able to convey even the most negative messages without giving discomfort or hopelessness to others. He knew how to negotiate in an effective way where the two sides were aware of their position, Joe said.

To understand his partner, Luong had talks with Joe over a glass of wine in a bar in Washington until mid-night. When the US negotiation delegation visited Hanoi, Luong took Joe and other US negotiators to a floating restaurant on the West Lake. "They were opportunities for us to relax and exchange views informally," Joe said.

To enrich his knowledge about modern international trade, Luong and his colleagues mulled over hundreds of legal documents of the WTO. Through the five years of negotiations, his life was associated with chapters, articles and numerous documents on international trade law. Whenever he left the negotiating table, Luong returned to his room at the headquarters of the Trade Ministry and worked without a day off.

Luong said "To negotiate with the US, I had to understand the unpredictable partner. I, therefore, had to gain knowledge. I would have to leave the negotiating table if I had no knowledge. A power, the US has no time to spend months gossiping."

Serene like a plowman

In May 1998, Luong and his colleagues handed over a re-outlined draft agreement to the US side, which was based on principles and rules of GATT/WTO and different from the document the US had given to Vietnam in April 1997 in many points, including the chapter on services and other clauses.

The US side was astonished as Vietnam rejected its draft agreement that had been signed by other countries in 1997. However, the US still accepted this since Vietnam had a point.

US chief negotiator Joe Damond told Luong that: "We are so surprised by Vietnam's progress…, having a partner like Vietnam, we feel joyful."

On the day when the deal was reached, Luong felt as if a huge burden had been lifted. "Following the signing, I returned to the Vietnamese Trade Office in Washington, with a feeling of serenity." The man pictured himself a plowman who enjoyed smoking after finishing his ploughing, after the five-year marathon for the BTA ended.

"Match-maker" of Vietnam-US relations

'Thanks to her good relations with US authorities and her beauty, gentleness and dynamism, Ginny played a special role in the normalization of the economic and trade ties between the two countries".

Xuan Danh (Young People – June 1, 2006)

At the signing ceremony of the BTA in the White House in the late spring of 2000, a woman went to a quiet corner, trying to hide her tears of joy. President of the US-Vietnam Trade Council (USVTC) Virginia Foote, who is called "Ginny" by her Vietnamese and American colleagues, experienced unforgettable moments in her life.

Falling in love with Vietnam

She hosted us in a small room with a large picture of Vietnam's former Foreign Minister Nguyen Co Thach and US Ambassador to the United Nations Bill Sullivan at the Council's headquarters in Hanoi. The beautiful, petite woman, born in the Northeast of the US, reminisced: "I visited Vietnam for the first time in 1989, together with other Congress members like Senators John McCain and John Kerry. However, the visit to Hanoi together with Ambassador Sullivan was my most memorable trip." She continued: "We had an unforgettable dinner at the Government Guest House. There was a power outage in Hanoi on the stormy day. We talked in the darkness until candles were lit. But no one seemed to notice it. As the two old friends, Minister Thach and Ambassador Sullivan chatted and laughed, and even asked each other about marriages and careers of their children."

Since then, her life has been closely associated with the normalization of the Vietnam-US relations. She travelled between Washington and Hanoi every few months, even monthly. She had a hectic schedule. When in Hanoi, she visited ministries and agencies, and met with local authorities. She conveyed messages of each side to the other, helping to increase their mutual understanding and press ahead with the normalization.

When in the US, the smart woman joined tens of congressional hearings to back the normalization of the Vietnam-US ties. Addressing the Congress, she stressed: "Vietnam and US shared a special history, but both have made all-out efforts to build a new future. We should look at Vietnam in many aspects and regularly assess the country's development."

"Following the normalization of the bilateral relations, she, in her capacity as President of the US-Vietnam Trade Council (USVTC), significantly contributed to the negotiations of the US-Vietnam Bilateral Trade Agreement (BTA). Thanks to her good relations with US authorities and her dynamism, Ginny played a special role in the normalization of the economic and trade ties between the two countries. She called for US firms' contributions to continuously organize workshops that offered the Vietnamese side insight into regulations and rules of the US and the world. Ginny also provided the Vietnamese negotiation delegation updates on different opinions raised at the US congressional hearings on the BTA, and response of US firms in different periods of time and negotiation rounds, helping the Vietnamese delegation acknowledge advantages and difficulties, as well as requirements from the US partner," said Nguyen Dinh Luong, Vietnam's chief negotiator for the BTA.

Close ties with Vietnam

Although the woman spent 17 years working with Vietnam, not all people know what she has done. Nguyen Dinh Luong said: "She deserves the highest reward for her great contributions to the development of the Vietnam-US relations." She can't count how many days she stayed in Vietnam, and how many flights between the US and the Southeast Asian country she took. She also can't remember how many leaders and officials she met in both Washington and Hanoi, in her efforts to bring the two nations closer. Ginny was present at almost all events during the normalization process. She witnessed ups and downs in the bilateral relations. Her mind is still filled with memories and events. "Another unforgettable experience is my trip to Vietnam together with President Clinton, during which I could clearly feel the US leader's love for the country. After Clinton visited Vietnam, my 84-year-old father decided to come there. Although I was worried to take my old father on the far journey, I finally satisfied his wish. This was an important decision. Through the trip, my father would know what his daughter had done in the country. He was very satisfied with the trip and six months later he passed away. For my father, it was an unforgettable trip" Ginny said, her eyes filling with tears.

"I also have good Vietnamese friends. Once I was severely ill, apart from my parents and daughter, a Vietnamese friend – Ambassador Le Bang – stayed with me until I got better."

Responding to our question regarding the lesson for Vietnam and the US through the signing of the BTA, Ginny said: "Many people have asked me the same question. I was most regretful about the chance we missed to reach the agreement although we were close to signing it, and two and a half years we wasted for a reason that was not worth as compared with the deal's significance to the Vietnamese economy and the US business community. Many blamed Vietnam for the delay, while others said the US was accountable. But I think that both of them had to pay dearly. I suggested weighing up benefits of opening door to the bilateral ties. Once the door is closed, we would have no opportunities to move ahead."

Sharing her view on the Vietnam-US relations in the next five years, Ginny said "Vietnam will join the World Trade Organization (WTO) and benefit from the US's Permanent Normal Trade Relations. The bilateral ties will develop more intensively and extensively in all channels. A bright future is what I believe in." And we can see it in her sparkling eyes.

Virginia Foote and the USVTC organized and contributed to more than 40 visits to Vietnam by US delegations, and vice versa.

Virginia Foote is now President and Co-founder of the USVTC, established in 1989 according to the suggestion of the Vietnamese Foreign Minister Nguyen Co Thach. The council pioneered the normalization of the Vietnam-US relations. Its educational forum provided technical support for Vietnam during the negotiations of the BTA. It is actively helping Vietnam with the implementation of the deal and joining the WTO. She has also recently been elected as Executive Vice President of the US-ASEAN Business Council.

Alleviating misunderstanding - building trust

"Vietnam shouldn't consider poverty and underdevelopment as reasons for delaying market opening, but should regard market closure as a cause of poverty and underdevelopment".

Huynh Phan (Vietnamnet – December 20, 2011)

The biggest difference from the US Chief negotiator Joe Damond was that he was not part of the "Vietnam War" generation, thus his research and approach towards the normalization of the trade ties between Vietnam and the US remained different, not to say totally fresh.

What did you think about your appointment as US chief negotiator for the BTA, as well as Vietnam?

Damond: I had little idea about Vietnam. When I was appointed as the US chief negotiator, I tried to ask for information from agencies, even US think-tanks. However, what I received was not very helpful. Only a few people knew about the country, but mainly military or issues regarding the war in Vietnam. When the two countries began normalizing their economic and trade ties, the two-way trade still remained modest, and the US's investment in Vietnam was even less than that.

I had thought the negotiation process would face a range of difficulties. However, when we embarked on the negotiations, I recognized similarities from the Vietnamese side. They also knew little about the trade relations with the US. Vietnam had signed a number of bilateral trade agreements, which, however, were totally different from the BTA.

I only believed at that time that the US should reach a trade agreement with Vietnam, as the war ended 20 years ago, and Vietnam had the potential of an emerging market. Vietnam also needed to access the US market to develop further.

Why were you assigned as US chief negotiator?

Damond: At that time, I was in charge of Southeast Asia at the US Trade Representative (USTR). I had experience in addressing trade issues with Thailand, Indonesia or Malaysia. When the decision on the BTA negotiations was issued, Charlene Barshefsky (US Chief Trade Representative) told me: "You are in charge of ASEAN, so you will be the chief negotiator for the BTA with Vietnam."

There was another reason which was a bit funny. My direct boss, who was in charge of entire ASEAN, refused to take on this position, saying he witnessed the Vietnam War, so he will not intervene in Vietnam's story. He then asked me to be head of the negotiation team."

Had you met any Vietnamese before?

Damond: I first came into contact with Vietnamese in December 1995 when I was part of a major delegation to Vietnam, led by Al Larson, Under Secretary of State for Economics, to discuss economic issues. There were different aspects regarding the normalization of the economic relations, such as the credit program of Eximbank, OPIC, and trade ties. During the visit, the two sides only looked into fields that needed mutual support.

What was difference between the talks between Henry Kissinger and Le Duc Tho, and the talks between Joseph Damond and Nguyen Dinh Luong?

Damond: During the negotiations in Paris, the Vietnamese side could wait and find ways to "kill time" as they were aware of the US's intention to withdraw from Vietnam.

However, the negotiations in Hanoi and Washington were contrary. We could wait as it would take Vietnam a long time to become an important market of the US. Meanwhile, Vietnam, particularly Luong's team, wanted to reach the agreement soon to access the US market to serve its national economic development.

Morever, I was still young and I could wait for another one or two years to resume the negotiations. Meanwhile, waiting was much more difficult for the old Vietnamese partner.

What was the lesson you learnt from the negotiations between Le Duc Tho and Kissinger?

Damond: Tho persistently asked the US side to contribute US$3.25 billion to healing war wounds and post-war reconstruction. Kissinger was forced to make the commitment, so he sought ways to add it to a diplomatic note of President Nixon. The implementation, at last, depended on the Congress.

Is feasibility the most important to a signed agreement?

Damond: That was one of the things Luong reminded us. The Vietnamese side wanted to affirm that they really understood the US's requirements. Signing the BTA so that Vietnam would benefit from the Normal Trade Relations from the US side was the easiest. However, the negotiations lasted longer, as both of us wanted to make sure that we understood the commitments, and we firmly believed in our implementation capacity.

How did you picture your partner before the negotiations?

Is it a negotiator similar to Le Duc Tho - the one who Kissinger wished not to meet again at the negotiating table, as he wrote in his memoirs, because Tho always harshly criticized him, even making him lose face?

Damond: (burst out laughing) I had no idea about the history of the negotiations. What I got was only through Kissinger's book featuring the negotiation process, exactly the period when the talks were about to be concluded. I didn't want to be haunted by the wartime past and feel guilty of the past. I am not sure whether that is right or wrong. But I think that many people have been living with the burden of the past in Vietnam. I am still young and I am lucky as I don't have such painful memories.

In the new era, I should understand Vietnam through my own experiences and have my own opinions on the country.

However, I still wondered why Luong, who experienced the war and studied in the former Soviet Union that had a centralized economy, would reach such a trade agreement that is based on market institutions.

And how about reality?

Damond: I think Luong was very frank and open. He told me about the problems that Vietnam had encountered so that I could understand and the negotiation could make progress.

The second thing he told me was that the Vietnamese negotiation delegation included many ministries.

Luong also told me not to talk in the diplomatic style because it would make Vietnam find it difficult to grasp the U.S's stance.

What surprised me most was that we built a people to people relationship between the two negotiators. He told me that he represented his country's system and wanted negotiation to evolve. But to achieve this, he required the United States to do it in this way, or in that way. He did not explain it to me in detail, but assured me that this was a necessary tactic to achieve progress from Vietnam.

And you believed?

Damond: Yes. He told the truth.

If it hadn't been Luong but another person, it would have possibly been a very tough stance and an attitude overwhelming people sitting opposite, especially a young person like me, only 33-34 years old. Moreover, since the Paris Agreement, Vietnam had been famous for its extremely tough negotiators.

But Luong was completely different from what I had imagined. He didn't "play games" during the negotiation, but he was very frank and required the same from me.

The second thing that surprised me was that an experienced man like him, supposed to be very strict, but he was so easy-going. He seemed to be a moderator and requested each member of his delegation to raise questions for the United States. Unlike me, a "dictator" who always tried to control my delegation and negotiation from the United States at the highest level.

Another point was that when I posed a question, or voiced my stance, he never said "Damond said this, asked that", he used "the U.S side" instead. Later, I could understand his wise way of speaking helped to reduce any bad impression of the Vietnamese negotiation delegation on me.

In your opinion, what were the fundamental differences between the two trade systems based on the Soviet model and GATT (General Agreement on Tariffs and Trade) as well as WTO?

Damond: We just set out the rules of the games and opened the market. However, we didn't impose how much each side's export volume would be. That was a fundamental difference between our BTA and the ones that Vietnam had signed with socialist countries.

Did it mean that the Agreement featured rules of the game which were identified and as fair as possible, while, its score depended on each side's efforts and was not pre-arranged as the ones in Vietnam's previous games with Comecon countries?

Damond: Exactly. And luckily, my initial suspicions were wrong. Luong understood this and also comprehended that Vietnam had to learn how to play by new rules, based on WTO's principles. Because the Soviet Union and Eastern European socialist system collapsed, it meant that the trade system they established no longer existed.

During the workshop to celebrate the 10th anniversary of implementing the Vietnam-U.S BTA, Luong said that the BTA was completely new to both Vietnam and the United States. With Vietnam, it was clear, but, why it was the same with the United States?

Damond: Firstly, the United States has granted most countries most-favored nation status (later changed into normal trade relations - NTR) on the basis of multilateral negotiations, not bilateral ones.

The United States has only signed the bilateral BTAs with China, the Soviet Union, Poland, and the Czech Republic. These BTAs were signed before 1994, when the Uruguay Round ended so that WTO supplanted GATT in 1995. The establishment of WTO has considerably changed the global trade system with new concepts of trade services, intellectual property rights, among others.

When Vietnam decided to negotiate BTA with the United States, they learned about the above-mentioned BTAs and realized that much content was added.

Luong said among BTAs that the United States signed with socialist countries, he liked the one with China (signed in 1979) most. How did you respond?

Damond: I remember I said that the BTA with China was even simpler than the one with the Soviet Union in 1991. I told Luong that the global trade locomotive was running, if wanting to get on, Vietnam had to catch it in the middle of the journey, and if wanting to get on at the first station, they would never catch this train.

Another important point was that when signing with China, within the framework of the Nixon-Kissinger strategy, Americans didn't think that China would later become an economic threat to the country. During the 90s, China emerged as a major power, along with Southeast Asia, South Korea and Japan. During the mid-1990s, the United States posted a trade deficit with Japan, while, China's goods were seen everywhere in the United States.

Therefore, since the 90s, the United States has become very serious in negotiating and signing trade agreements, in its trade policies in general.

Did Vietnam accept that explanation?

Damond: Vietnam's reaction that I remember most was Luong's response, saying that the United States was tough with his country due to historical issues.

I explained that it wasn't related to the past, that I didn't know about and wasn't interested in this history. But, the important thing here was 130 WTO countries members at that time accepted the organization's principles, so, the U.S-Vietnam trade ties weren't an exception. Vietnam should accept most of those principles.

Vietnam wanted the United States to accept to treat it as a young country, needing time to grow up, before accepting to treat it as an adult. It meant that the country wanted to wait for the negotiation to join WTO.

The U.S viewpoint was that this was a win-win story, hence, if the United States opened the market to Vietnam, the latter must also do that. If the United States gained no benefits from

Vietnam, there would be no way the U.S Congress would adopt it.

Was the first design of negotiation content put forward by the United States?

Damond: That's right. Luong required the United States to create it. The first design was short, only about 3-4 pages, but it covered all fields that we planned to negotiate.

My initial negotiating strategy was that the two sides would negotiate each area before reaching a complete agreement. But Luong said that way would not suit Vietnam. He said Vietnam would not be able to understand in such a general way, they needed to receive specific requirements from the United States such as tariff rates.

I said that Luong's request completely went against my negotiating viewpoint because I didn't want the United States to be an imposer.

How did Luong explain?

Damond: Luong said he needed to do that to report to the Vietnamese government that the United States had requested them this and that. I understood Luong needed to do that for the internal story and we spent several months on working with USTR's attorneys to combine contents of BTAs which the United States signed earlier with new commitments included in WTO.

And that was a basis for us to keep on negotiating.

When you gave the first design to Vietnam, how did Luong react?

Damond: In a letter sent to me later, Luong, but I thought it was the Vietnamese government's stance, said Vietnam was a poor and underdeveloped country and could only accept international standards (WTO) by 2020.

I responded that (I actually don't remember whether in a letter or in negotiation), we couldn't wait until 2020, it meant 23 years more. However, the second thing was important.

I said: "You say Vietnam is a poor and underdeveloped country. Yes, the reason that makes Vietnam poor and underdeveloped is the fact that the country hasn't opened its market to the world, it means that it hasn't become a part of the global economy. Vietnam shouldn't consider poverty and underdevelopment as reasons for delaying market opening, but should regard market closure as a cause of poverty and underdevelopment".

We discussed again and again, and seemed still not to understand each other. The negotiation made no progress until I received a fax in early 1998.

Who sent you that fax and what was its contents?

Damond: On the first working day of New Year 1998, after the Christmas holiday, I received a fax, because there was no Internet back then. It was a letter from Luong, about 5-6 pages or so. In the letter, Luong clearly and generally stated the steps that Vietnam would take.

After reading the letter, I understood that we could continue negotiating to sign an agreement.

Was that the turning point of the negotiation?

Damond: That's right. I was really surprised when reading that letter. Although Ginny Foote and Dan Price, Luong's consultants had told me that I could hope from Vietnam for a completely different approach.

I know Ginny Foote. What role did Dan Price play in the negotiation process?

Damond: Ginny was so wise in introducing Dan to Luong. I know Dan well because he worked with me at USTR, of course in a more senior position than me. Dan is a wonderful person as he has lots of experience in negotiating BTA with the Soviet Union.

For example, at first, the United States would only accept if Vietnam was informed of our roadmap in opening markets in the country.

Of course I knew, but I couldn't tell them, simply because I didn't negotiate for the sake of Vietnam. Vietnam must "set a price" first, and then I will "pay the price".

Dan's appearance was really timely. Dan understood at which level of the opening roadmap the United States would accept as well as give a good consultation to Vietnam.

Another thing that surprised me was how Luong and Dan were able to persuade the relevant Vietnamese ministries to agree with the draft.

Well, there's one thing, though you didn't ask, on which I still want to express my opinion. That is, after sending me the design of negotiation content, Tuyen and Luong continued to explain and persuade within the Vietnam delegation to reach consensus.

How did you know?

Damond: They sent me a letter, requesting me to assert that the United States would only negotiate with Vietnam substantively by using the recent design. I understood my response letter would be a supporting document for them to persuade the Vietnamese Government.

This is the first time that I have heard such a story.

Damond: I still think Luong was reluctant to approach it this way to achieve the goal. He required me to be strong and firm to voice my stance with the Vietnamese negotiating delegation.

Did it mean that through you, Luong wanted to "stimulate" people behind to be active?

Damond: Exactly. At least I felt it clearly. Thanks to that, Vietnam resumed negotiation in May 1998 with a much better proposal.

There was another important detail needing a mention. In the summer of 1997, the Vietnamese Ministry of Trade dispatched a team to Geneva (Switzerland) to work with a specialized group of WTO secretariat to learn about the organization. Nguyen Hong Duong, lawyer of the Vietnamese negotiation delegation, Luong's son-in-law, was part of the team sent to Geneva. After returning, they became professional experts. I even couldn't answer some of their questions on the spot and needed to look up documents later.

Since that time, they had come to understand the information we gave. Of which, the most important thing was that the standards were not American, but were WTO ones.

While Vietnam- United States were negotiating the BTA, China negotiated with the United States about joining the WTO. Did you keep a watch on that process?

Damond: Yes. The division in charge of negotiation with China worked at USTR, right next to my office, so, I learned a lot from them.

What did you learn?

Damond: Vietnamese and Chinese economies are similar, because they are in the socialist economic system. However, Vietnam is left behind a long way compared to China.

I will give an example.

One of the obstacles in U.S- Vietnam negotiation was trading and distribution rights. Only state-owned enterprises monopolize trade in Vietnam.

Colleagues in charge of negotiation with China showed me a three-page document on what they had negotiated with the country on such trading rights.

After reading it, I exclaimed: "It is completely similar to what I am doing with Vietnam, and I can use it to adjust my plan".

When Vietnam negotiated to join the WTO, did it make efforts to protect trading and distribution rights for its state-owned enterprises?

Damond: Yes, it did. I found it most difficult to negotiate with Vietnam in those two points. There was a long list of areas needed to be liberalized to get the trading rights in the Agreement. Of course, we separated the distribution rights.

We accepted concessions because we wanted the Agreement to be feasible, but not for all fields. There is the field which can be done in ten years, but there is another can be done in 5 years, or even 2.

In September 1999, who informed you that the Agreement wouldn't be signed in Aukland?

Damond: While sitting at the hotel's suite, where Luong and I worked together on the documents, I received a phone call from the Embassy in Hanoi saying that the Agreement wouldn't be signed.

How did you feel at that time?

Damond: I was really shocked.

I went out to tell Luong about the phone call.

Luong didn't know. He said that Tuyen had just landed an hour ago, and he would call Minister Tuyen to cross-check.

He then sighed and said, "You're right."

Did you think Luong really didn't know when you informed him?

Damond: I'm sure he didn't know. Because I closely followed changes in his facial expressions while he was calling Tuyen.

Was President Clinton informed that the Agreement would be signed in Auckland, and would he witness that historic moment?

Damond: Yes, he was. I talked to the White House about the signing ceremony.

I looked forward to being with President Clinton in the great event, like nothing I had ever attended before.

I imagined I would turn over pages for the U.S. Trade Representative Barshefsky to sign, while, President Clinton behind would keep a close watch on my gestures.

Did you anticipate President Clinton's reaction when it was announced that the event he was looking forward to finish the relation normalization process with Vietnam, from diplomacy to trade, initiated by him and witnessed by heads of 20 APEC economies, was postponed?

Damond: No.

When did you know the reasons behind the suspension of the signing?

Damond: All we knew was that Hanoi didn't reach a final consensus. There were Vietnamese leaders objecting at the last minute that it wasn't an appropriate time to sign the BTA with the United States.

At the workshop on the occasion of the 10th anniversary of enforcement of the BTA (December 9, 2011), you said you thought that it would take more 5 years to renegotiate from scratch. Were you really afraid of that?

Damond: I was afraid that they would invite Luong and said "Tuyen and you gave the United States too much, and your duty now is claiming it back".

Does it mean wiping chessboard out and starting over?

Damond: I was afraid so.

In your sense, what was the main cause?

Damond: I really had no idea what happened. Nevertheless, I supposed that something occurred during Secretary of State Madeleine Albright's visit to Hanoi to attend APEC. She must have said something that made the Vietnamese leaders reconsider to sign the BTA with the United States, because the preparation for the signing was almost complete.

At that workshop, Luong and I asserted that it would take us only half an hour to resolve the remaining 12 technical provisions during our meeting in Washington DC in July, 2020.

But if that's all, why were you afraid that the negotiation would start from scratch and last for another 5 years?

Damond: I guessed that there were Vietnamese leaders still not wanting to open the market to the United States. They took the occasion to condemn Luong and Tuyen for their unacceptable concessions.

Within 10 months between Auckland and Washington, did you hold discussions with Luong?

Damond: Much later. At first, we decided that whether they would sign or not depended on them. We didn't want to talk about this again.

Luong sent me a letter to invite me to Hanoi in mid-March. I really wanted to go to discuss with Luong ways to save the Agreement on which the two of us and the negotiation delegations had spent efforts for many years, although it was only about the technical issues.

However, Barshefsky and her Assistant Fisher and Ambassador Peterson didn't allow me to come to Vietnam. They said that the U.S Chief Negotiator coming to Vietnam would be a signal of the United States being ready to renegotiate.

Indeed, during that time, I was very confused. I didn't know what to do, although I really wanted to do something.

How was the deadlock broken, in order that the two sides signed the Agreement four months later?

Damond: It was the role of Ginny Foote. Dan Price came to Hanoi and everything became clearer. In July 2000, Luong went to Washington DC with Vu Khoan, who replaced Truong Dinh Tuyen from the Trade Ministry. I understood that everything was OK.

After the signing of the BTA, would you continue working for USTR?

Damond: Just one more year.

Why?

Damond: I was lucky to sign a very important and historic Agreement. I had the chance to step in the White House and shook hands with the U.S President.

I don't think that luck would appear twice. Thus, I decided to leave USTR to seek new challenges. That was also the reason why I wrote the memoirs of the BTA negotiation.

I wanted the entire past preserved in the book, instead of following me on the path I am going, before handing it over to my children so that they can learn more about my memorable time. It's so happy to imagine that moment, when I become older.

When will the memoir be published?

Damond: Hopefully next year. Luong and I came to the World Publishing House to work with them.

Has the English version been published in the United States yet?

Damond: Not yet. Hopefully it will be printed in the United States, after being released in Vietnam.

{Ambassador "Pete" Douglas Peterson told the author in July 2010, on the sidelines of the workshop held in Hanoi to celebrate the 10th anniversary of the normalization of Vietnam-U.S diplomatic relations:

In Spring 2000, when Vietnam sent a signal to the United States for resuming negotiation, the U.S side wanted to wait for more time to confirm the Vietnam's certain desire to sign the BTA with the US.

The BTA's slow signing caused Vietnam 2 wasted years to re-start the negotiation of joining WTO, therefore, the country missed the boat to enter the WTO earlier. Moreover, when Vietnam started the bilateral negotiation for really joining WTO (in 2004), the country had to meet higher standard requirements, and it meant that Vietnam had to make more commitments.}

PART 2

STILL VALUABLE LESSONS

Vietnam – US: What foundation for the game?

"I cannot imagine how the US "Pivot to Asia" policy would be without the Vietnam factor, while Vietnam is advocating for diversification and multilateralization in relations, and also needs to gather forces, find peace to develop, in an unstable world" - Nguyen Dinh Luong (Vietnamnet – March 2, 2015)

Prior to General Secretary Nguyen Phu Trong's visit to the United States, Nguyen Dinh Luong, former Chief Negotiator of the Vietnam – US Bilateral Trade Agreement, discussed on Tuan Viet Nam (Vietnam Week) the milestones in the relations between the two countries during the 20 years after normalizing relations.

For mutual interests

Over the past twenty years, Vietnam-US relations have rapidly developed in both breadth and depth and have now become a comprehensive partnership.

Like every other relation in the international arena, the Vietnam - US relations are governed by the interests of both parties. Let us take a look at the history.

In 1873, Bui Vien crossed the waves of the Pacific Ocean to reach Washington, waited a whole year to meet the US President to ask for help in the fight against the French. At the meeting, the US President welcomed the idea immediately, because at that time the US and France were at war in

Mexico. Unfortunately, Bui Vien did not bring his letter of credentials, so he had to come back empty-handed. But when Bui Vien returned with the letter, the US was no longer interested because the US-French war in Mexico had ended. The two countries no longer had common interests.

In 1945 and 1946, President Ho Chi Minh sent 11 letters and telegrams to the US President and Secretary of State, proposing the US to support Vietnam's independence and establish comprehensive relations between the two countries. But he received no reply because Vietnam did not appear on the US screen of interests, or maybe the US was not interested because it was obscured by the image of interests with other powers.

It was not until 1995 that the two countries could normalize diplomatic relations. Only one year after relations normalization, the United States actively started negotiating a Bilateral Trade Agreement (BTA) and Vietnam responded immediately, because both sides needed, wanted, and saw the benefits in the Agreement.

When negotiating the BTA, the first US Ambassador to Vietnam Pete Peterson said he hoped that once we had the BTA, Vietnam's exports to the United States would increase to 5-6 billion US dollars, too big a number for Vietnam at that time which no one could imagine. The Ambassador did not predict a specific timeline.

However, after only 2 years of implementing the BTA, Vietnam's exports to the US had reached that number, and in 2014 the figures reached more than USD 18 billion, which was more than 3 times higher than Peterson's expectation.

The United States is always Vietnam's largest export market and also the largest export surplus market.

Everyone can see that Vietnam clearly gains benefits, as do the US. American consumers who have a wider choice of goods. The US market also has an increasingly strong competitor, contributing to raising the US economy's overall competitiveness.

Moreover, for a 10-to-15-dollar shirt produced in Vietnam, Vietnam only gets 4-5 dollars in wages, while the shirt is sold at 80-100 dollars in the US market. The production cost of a pair of sport shoes in Vietnam is about 10-20% of its selling price in the US market.

This means that both sides gain benefits. No one can calculate which side gains more advantages, yet in the game, the more clever are the more successful.

The better this benefit grows, the further economic and trade relations develop.

Benefits create their own games

In international politics, gathering of powers is currently actively taking place. Those who have the need to gather power in Asia (and in the world) must not leave out Vietnam, due to its geopolitical position. And that includes the United States. The United States certainly does not want to exclude Vietnam from its regional efforts, much less they do want to let Vietnam hamper that strategy. It is Vietnam's geopolitical position that is forcing the Americans to step by step commit to deepening cooperation in many fields.

I cannot imagine how the US "Pivot to Asia" policy would be if they leave out the Vietnam factor, while Vietnam is advocating for diversification and multilateralization in relations, and also needs to build partnerships, find peace to develop, in an unstable world.

The more the benefits increase, the deeper and more extensive cooperation is required. That is also the inevitable substance of the future development steps in Vietnam - US relations.

When the benefits are large enough, each side knows how to control and close the gaps to open up cooperation. If the United States wants to entice Vietnam, it must soften its human rights claims. If Vietnam wants to play with the US, it has to put aside differences, for example, those that are happening in the TPP negotiations.

There are times when global and regional political and social upheavals affect relations between countries. For example, developments in the South China Sea seem to have brought the US closer to Vietnam and accelerated the relaxation of the US embargo on lethal weapons.

In the summary conclusions of a conference named "Vietnam – United States relationship: For 20 more successful years", which took place recently in Hanoi, the President of the Diplomatic Academy of Vietnam Dang Dinh Quy, the organizer and chairperson of the conference, made many insightful and interesting comments. Among them, I would like to requote a comment: The interests of Vietnam and the United States not only lie in bilateral relations but also in cooperation between the two countries in larger frameworks such as ASEAN, AFTA, as well as many other international organizations.

For example, the US "Pivot to Asia" policy cannot fail to take ASEAN into account. The United States considers the unity and strength of ASEAN as one of its interests, and Vietnam is an active member, sincerely wishing to contribute to the growth, unity and solidarity in the ASEAN. Therefore, the cooperation between the United States and Vietnam in the region is significantly necessary and useful.

The Trans-Pacific Partnership negotiation has one good point, which is the package negotiation (not negotiating separate issue) and a multilateral negotiation, a collective of 12 countries, for which the United States is considered the host. That approach will help to solve a series of problems that cannot be solved in bilateral negotiations.

Sensitive issues to Vietnam include freedom of association, transparency and publicity in the operations of state-owned enterprises, publicity and equality in public procurement, in the access to capital, natural resources, and markets. When negotiating the BTA, the United States had already raised these issues but Vietnam resolutely refused to accept. In this negotiation, which is a   collective process, most of the participating countries have already accepted these terms. In order to complete the negotiations, Vietnam must have plans to take a step back and then amend the law to match its commitments.

Despite such difficulties and complications, Vietnam is still eager to participate in, and the United States wants Vietnam to participate. Among Southeast Asian countries, besides Brunei, Singapore and Malaysia, which voluntarily participated in from the beginning, the United States did not invite anyone but Vietnam. Maybe because Americans think it is better that Vietnam plays with the United States.

Moreover, inviting Vietnam to join the TPP means pulling Vietnam closer into the vibrant market economy and imperceptibly forcing Vietnam to cut off the legacies from a subsidized bureaucratic economy. Those legacies both make Vietnam's economy less efficient and maintain an unclear legal environment that can tolerate corruption, making foreign investors, including the US investors afraid to invest in the Vietnamese market.

And why is Vietnam so enthusiastic? Economic pressure is forcing Vietnam to be enthusiastic, and if it does not break through, the Vietnamese economy will fall behind and will definitely fall into the middle-income trap.

Participating in the TPP is a wise decision, a brave action to create a breakthrough, to strengthen the pressure to continue the inside reform process.

Hoang Ngoc recorded

Common rules of game will help us grow up

(Remarks at a seminar on reviewing and comparing current Vietnamese laws with the Vietnam-US Bilateral Trade Agreement. Hanoi, 2005)

"Vietnamese officials do not easily break the habit of treating enterprises as controlled entities by them, not as their partners." - Nguyen Dinh Luong

I would like to thank the Organization Committee for handing me a chance to participate in this valuable seminar.

I am really grateful for the responsible activities, the respectable patience and perseverance of independent legal experts who are members of the Review Team, experts of the START project under the Ministry of Justice on the process of reviewing legal documents of Vietnam, comparing and differentiating with regulations and commitments in the Vietnam - US Bilateral Trade Agreement (BTA) and the provisions of the WTO in the period I, which was in 2001 and period II, which is currently happening.

I completely agree with the objectives, requirements, scope of the review as well as the evaluations, comments, suggestions and recommendations that you have carefully prepared.

As the person who has the luck to have the longest and deepest involvement in the process of preparation, in development of negotiation plan and in negotiation of the BTA, I would like to make a few comments for your reference. Those comments are general, not just trade related ones.

Vietnam is reviewing the law and comparing it with the commitments in the BTA, so what is the BTA?

BTA - The Vietnam - US Bilateral Trade Agreement is a specific product (viewed from many angles) of the specific relationship between Vietnam and the US.

The history of relations between the two countries leaves too many problems that need to be solved. The United States treats Vietnam like no other country. Vietnam views the United States also like no other country.

One year after normalizing relations, the two countries decided to start negotiating to normalize economic and trade relations, while the whole world was being pulled into economic globalization and free trade, while the two "former foes" had not yet understood each other and trusted each other, especially had not yet understood each other's economic laws and policies. In that context, both sides had the desire to negotiate and sign an agreement that is very strict, very diligent, to the maximum extent.

From the beginning, the US side had the intention to negotiate and sign a Comprehensive Agreement with all necessary contents according to WTO standards. Vietnam had previously applied to join the WTO, ready to negotiate an agreement under the WTO, as long as the commitments did not harm Vietnam's interests.

In fact, as a rule, the BTA is just a legal framework that regulates trade between two countries, meanwhile, the Vietnam - US BTA is stuffed with all sorts of detail, such as:

Chapter II: Intellectual property rights (IPR)

Vietnam and the United States could have signed a separate agreement on intellectual property rights. The US did the same thing with China and some other nations. The United States also thought that piracy and intellectual property violations in Vietnam were still common. Currently, Vietnam's laws in this area are still too poor, so it's best to put intellectual property in the BTA to be sure.

The Vietnam side had no convincing reason to refuse that request. The country must both accept and take this opportunity to improve the domestic situation in the country. If it did not improve the intellectual property violation situation, foreign investment would not have come in, especially in technology investment fields. Vietnam also needed this opportunity to strengthen its domestic intellectual property protection system. If it did not accept the request at that time, it would have had to accept this when entering the WTO.

Chapter IV: Development of Investment Relations

Among 15 articles in chapter IV, only Article 11 - "Trade - Related Investment Measures" is directly related to the WTO, in its TRIMS Agreement. The other 14 are either unrelated or just indirectly related.

Vietnam and the United States could have signed a separate investment protection agreement with each other like the way Vietnam and the United States had done with many other countries. But the US side believed that Vietnam's investment law at that time was not transparent and detailed enough to protect US investors' interest, so they also decided to include the investment chapter in the BTA.

As for the Vietnam side, when deciding to normalize economic and trade relations with the United States, Vietnam had paid great attention to and hoped for a substantial source of investment from the US, therefore, Vietnam accepted, and also took the occasion to improve its investment environment, which already had many problems.

Chapter V: Business Facilitation

Commitments in this chapter have nothing to do with the WTO. They are simply problems that American businessmen operating business in Vietnam were caught in a complicated matrix of administrative procedures in Vietnam. On the occasion of the BTA negotiation, they asked the US negotiators to take action to remove it. Regarding the Vietnam side, the Vietnamese negotiators found that their demands were legitimate and not contrary to the laws. Putting them in the Agreement they also had "nothing to lose". Moreover, if they could be included in the Agreement as an international commitment, it would further accelerate the administrative reform process that had just started.

There were many other similar problems. All of the above situations created a particular BTA for a particular relationship at a particular time. And the Vietnam - US BTA was not the same as any BTA that the US had signed with other countries.

BTA was not yet the WTO

Commitments in the BTA were designed based on WTO principles or in the spirit of the WTO principles. It could be said that most of the basic WTO principles were properly expressed in the BTA. Fulfilling the BTA obligations meant fulfilling 65-70% of a WTO member's obligations.

The BTA was not yet the WTO because there are a number of other WTO contents and obligations that had not been mentioned in the BTA, and when negotiating to join the WTO, Vietnam must continue to address them.

For example, just in the field of trade, there are many WTO agreements that the BTA had not discussed or only touched on a little, such as Agreement on Subsidies, Agreement on Safeguards, Agreement on Import Licensing Procedures, Rules of Origin, Agreement on Pre-shipment Inspection, Agreement on the Application of Sanitary and Phytosanitary Measures, and Agreement on Agriculture. When trading with each other, countries cannot ignore the provisions in those agreements.

The fact that the BTA was not yet the WTO is also shown in Vietnam's minimal commitments to open the market. For example, the import tax in the BTA only reached 3.8% of the tariff lines in Vietnam's import tariff. When entering the WTO, Vietnam had to negotiate and commit to the entire tariff schedule. Vietnam's opening schedules in trade in goods and in services were still slow and lasted from 2 to 8 years. When negotiating the WTO, there probably would not be such a long route.

We were actively negotiating to join the WTO as soon as possible. When joining the WTO, Vietnam had to fully, seriously and unconditionally comply with the WTO's regulations. The WTO's policy review body would check the quality of Vietnam's legal documents and Vietnam's compliance with the WTO laws. Therefore, the thing that needed to be done, which actually should have been done a much earlier, was to review Vietnam's legal documents and compare them with WTO's provisions. That meant that independent legal experts as well as review team members could not think about taking a day off.

Legal document review in Vietnam is a difficult and complex task, which must be done regularly and constantly.

Why is it difficult?

Phase 1 of the general review of Vietnam's legal documents and comparisons with commitments in the BTA and the WTO provisions, which took place in 2001, helped Vietnam discover many valuable things. It was the differences between Vietnam's legal system and the global system, which exist in both nature and content, and in construction method, legal system structure, and application method.

While the world's laws are detailed, clear, easy to understand and easy to implement, Vietnamese laws are considered to be general, inconsistent, asynchronous, unclear and difficult to implement.

For example, the Commercial Law was issued in 1997. After nine years of existence, none of its provisions seem to have come into practice. Because the law was built on a commercial concept that was strange to the global one.

For example, on the Civil Code issued in October 1995, regarding intellectual property rights, there are 3 chapters and 80 articles (from 745 to 825) that fully cover all areas of intellectual property, (compared to TRIPS, it only lacked program-carrying signals transmitted by satellite), yet it did not protect any intellectual property, as it was it was publicly and obviously violated, and everyone could see the violations.

It is wonderful that our National Assembly has been adjusting, amending, and renewing the Vietnam's legal system.

But who can assure that, after this amendment, Vietnam's laws will become a unified, synchronized and stable legal system as required by the BTA and the WTO?

Who can assure that after this supplement, Vietnamese laws will eliminate all mistakes and defects?

Detecting errors is hard, correcting errors is even much harder. The struggle with the drafts of the general Law on Investment, the unified Law on Enterprises or the Decree guiding the implementation of the Competition Law, and the currently revised Commercial Law, says a lot. To implement the BTA, Vietnam has done a lot of work, but there is still a lot to be done. The work that has not yet been done is the most difficult part.

Why does it need to be regular and long-term? Because:

First, negotiations to join the WTO have not ended, and we have not seen all the things that we need to do.

About 2 weeks before, on Vietnamese television, the Managing Director of Ford Vietnam Limited complained that currently, Vietnamese auto companies were allowed to import completely built up (CBU) cars for domestic sale, while foreign auto companies were not. This is unequal and discriminatory. He asked Vietnam to allow Ford Motor Company to import CBU cars. Is the request of the Managing Director of Ford right or wrong and will Vietnam solve it?

The director's request has not been resolved because, based on the committed schedule in the BTA, it will take 9 to 10 years after the BTA implementation for joint ventures with the US to be allowed to import cars into Vietnam and sell in the country. However, he was right and his request will be resolved soon if in this WTO negotiation term, the Vietnam's negotiating team accepts most countries' pressure on demanding Vietnam to allow foreign-invested enterprises to exercise trade and distribution rights immediately after joining the WTO.

Second, Vietnamese officials do not easily break the habit of treating enterprises as objects of management, not as partners.

Nowadays, Vietnam can declare anywhere that the basic principle of transparency is consistent with the requirements of the BTA and the WTO. The State has issued Government's Decree No. 104/2004/ND-CP dated March 23, 2004 on the Official Gazette of the Socialist Republic of Vietnam for the organization and operation of the Provincial Official Gazette, and Joint Circular No. 04/2005/TTLT-TP-NV dated May 5, 2005 of the Ministry of Justice and Ministry of Home Affairs on guiding functions, tasks, powers and organization of specialized agencies to assist the People's Committee in state management of judicial work in the locality. That means the legal documents have been made public and transparent.

However, in fact, Vietnam itself cannot be confident, and does not dare to say that the principle of openness and transparency is guaranteed. When we listened to the Minister of Home Affairs report to the 10th National Assembly that a foreign ship that wanted to enter a Vietnam's port had to submit 28 different sets of documents, no one could explain why. When we listened to the Minister of Natural Resources and Environment report to the 10th National Assembly that to implement the Law on Land, there were more than 200 sub-law documents containing regulations on land management, not to mention regulations on land management included in the Civil Code, Criminal Code, Law on Agricultural Land Use. Moreover, according to the Tuoi Tre newspaper, on August 5, 2001, the Supreme People's Procuracy examined and discovered that, in 2000 alone, central (not to mention local) ministries and agencies issued 3,376 legal documents contrary to the law.

Third, there is still ignorance and intentional ignorance of the global rules.

1. Vietnam issued Ordinance No. 41/2002/PL-UBTVQH on May 25, 2002 on most favored nation and national treatment in international commerce. This is an important legal document aimed at unifying the State management of most-favored-nation (MFN) and national treatment (NT) on the basis of equality and mutual benefit in international trade. And today, Vietnam can declare to the world that in Vietnam there is equal treatment, no more discrimination.

What about the reality? The mentioned Ordinance has been designed using the method of extracting almost full relevant passages in the BTA for sufficiency in both spirit and content.

However, there has been no implementation guidelines issued due to its difficulty.

The more important the ordinance that is issued, the much more important for the principle of equal treatment to be thoroughly understood in all specialized legal documents of all branches at all levels, as well as have the principles practically applied.

If we do not continue to review to transpose the principles of MFN and NT in specialized legal documents, the Ordinance on MFN and NT will be just like a small drop of green oil on the surface of a basin of muddy water. The oil drop spreads making the water surface green, and we easily say the water has become pure green.

In reality, in Vietnam's market, state-owned and non-state-owned enterprises are playing on two different playing fields, domestic and foreign enterprises are also playing on separate playing fields.

2. You all know by heart that the MFN principle provides 3 exceptions, as do the BTA and WTO, with only 3 exceptions, which are advantages for others:

- In the customs alliances.

- In the free-trade zones.

- Facilitating border exchanges.

Vietnam and the EU signed the Textile and Garment Agreement. Vietnam reduces import tax on alcohol and motorcycles from the EU. This reduction on alcohol and motorbike taxes is clearly not one of the three exceptions mentioned above. If it is not in the exceptions, automatically other countries are entitled. However, Vietnam only pointed out a document applying to reduce taxes on alcohol and motorbikes to the EU. Then, because the US and Australia fought strongly, then another document was signed by Vietnam to reduce the tax on alcohol and motorbikes for the US and Australia, but other countries were not mentioned.

Ladies and gentlemen, I would like to end my talk with a thought, a suggestion:

Nowadays, in the information technology age, the Internet age, the era of economic globalization, the pathway we can choose to promote our country's development, to narrow the gap of lagging too far behind, even compared to the surrounding countries: is to integrate into the world economy. We must follow the general rules of the game in that playing field. Those common rules would help us grow and develop.

Chief Negotiator of the BTA delegation "Signing this agreement, we had nothing to lose"

"By the end of the negotiation, Mr. Peterson – The US Ambassador to Vietnam - said that the BTA would increase Vietnam's exports to the US by $ 6-8 billion. I didn't believe in it though. Nowadays, the turnover has been nearly $ 80 billion."

Dan Anh (NDH.vn - July 13, 2020)

- As the Chief Negotiator of the BTA, in retrospect of last 20 years, what are the benefits of this agreement in your point of view?

- Today, the relationship between Vietnam and the US has become a comprehensive partnership. Vietnam and America became friends. We escaped from former foes who didn't want to see each other, didn't trust each other, and it akin to a visceral dislike of each other, but we have shaken hands and cooperate in all fields today.

The core of this relationship is the economic relationship after the BTA. After the BTA signing, trade and cooperation have been strongly promoted. That produces many benefits and increases exchanges, Vietnamese people going to America and vice versa. The more people travel, the closer they get, the closer the relationship is to trust, understand and sympathy for each other; from economic benefit background to a rise in other interests in international forums. That is the development process.

- Can we can estimate those in detail, Sir?

I think not only me but many others also find it incredible in such rapid development of the bilateral trade ties. It is more clear to me as my lifetime has been associated with trade relations. I negotiated with Eastern European countries and the former Soviet Union in the Council for Mutual Economic Assistance, and joined talks for almost all agreements with the region, so I understand   domestic trade. At that time, Vietnam's annual export revenue to the former Soviet Union was about RUB1 billion, and the export value to Eastern European countries stood at 5-7 million, or 20-30 million. When signing the BTA, I forecasted that bilateral trade would increase, but didn't expect the sharp rise, now reaching nearly US$80 billion.

When the BTA negotiations began, Vietnam's GDP was only about US$30 billion, as compared with Coca-Cola's brand value of up to US$90 billion. A number of people said the US wanted to destroy the Vietnamese economy. I replied that we had nothing to lose. Twenty-years later, Vietnam's GDP was close to US$300 billion. Its export-import turnover also expanded to more than US$500 billion, which is the result of market opening.

During integration, countries were in the race to exploit the US market that dominated the global development. It was the US market that helped Japan to recover after the war, and spurred the development of the Republic of Korea (RoK) and Singapore. Once countries penetrated the US market, they must observe rules set by the country and followed by the entire world.

After the BTA was signed, businesses from the US, Europe and other Asian countries came to Vietnam. Given this, Vietnam tightened relations with not only the US but also other nations. It is the economic links that have contributed to enhancing relations between countries. Vietnam's strategic position has also played a role in the development of the Vietnam-US relationship. This affirms Vietnam's sound policy of multilateralization and diversification of relations. The country has optimized its advantages to grow further.

- How was the "pre-BTA" pressure as you said earlier?

There were different opinions in Vietnam at that time. The war has left a significant psychological impact. It was the most severe war in Vietnamese history, with millions of people killed and most villages ravaged. The two sides, therefore, distrusted each other. No Vietnamese cared about the US's most advanced economy that was dominating the global economy. I even humorously dubbed the US as "guardian" and anyone who wanted to join the World Trade Organization (WTO) must have his permission.

Given the shortage of documents, I had to collect information from different sources to find out how Japan and Singapore brought into full play the US market, and what Vietnam should do.

During a working trip to the central province of Quang Nam, I attended the inaugural ceremony of the Tam Ky Hall, which saw the participation of thousands of delegates, including war veterans. As Quang Nam is home to the largest number of heroic Vietnamese mothers, I offered incense to them, saying generations of Vietnamese always bear in mind their great contributions to the nation, and asking for their permission to launch a revolution to bring the country ahead. Vietnam would not make progress if we live with enmity. I saw the participating war veterans shaking their heads as a symbol of approval for my suggestion. There was huge pressure when proposing the signing of the BTA.

In a workshop organized at a time when the BTA was still under negotiation, a delegate suggested extending the talks. I replied: "Please take into account people's interests.' Even after the negotiations were concluded, there were still disapproval opinions.

-Had you ever thought that the BTA would not be signed due to such pressure?

Never. Because I had anticipated the difficulties and was determined to enrich my knowledge in this regard. No mistakes should be made during the talks. Over the past two decades, no mistakes have been found and no one said I was wrong. At that time, Vietnam was shifting from a centrally planned to a market economy, and had nothing to lose. It was hard to find documents on US culture and politics. I was a plowman, not a PhD, so I had to read different types of books to gain knowledge about the US.

The BTA was based on WTO rules. The US required mutual benefits during the negotiations. Vietnam needed to transform its centrally planned economy if it wanted to welcome the US. The transformation towards the market economy required the BTA to be designed on the basis of WTO rules. There were advantages to the BTA.

Vietnam has recently signed a number of new-generation free trade agreements, with the latest the Comprehensive and Progressive Agreement for Trans-Pacific Partnership (CPTPP) and the EU-Vietnam Free Trade Agreement (EVFTA). Such new-generation FTAs are the expansion and upgrade of the WTO whose rules which have been maintained since its inception in January 1995. The new FTAs are formed to meet requirements of the global economy that is developing more intensively and extensively. However, all of the commitments are based on the WTO. The global economy is still developing on the principles of equality, transparency, and the expansion of services and investment. Therefore, the BTA was outlined in accordance with the WTO. Vietnam has signed a range of agreements with many regions, notably CPTPP and EVFTA. Many have wondered whether Vietnam can optimize all of the deals. In my opinion differing from them, Vietnam would not move ahead if it had no links with other economies, and if the Vietnamese economy was not connected with global value chains. Therefore, the Party's policy of signing more agreements is totally sound.

-You just mentioned benefits. Which side do you think would benefit more from the BTA?

There was an article analyzing benefits for each side. I can take an example of a pair of shoes made in Vietnam, with 10-20 percent (about US$10-20) of its value created in the country, possibly from materials or workforce. Meanwhile, the product would be sold at a price of US$80-100 in the US, which may cover other costs like transportation and marketing. Therefore, it is hard to conclude which side gets more benefits from the BTA. Those who have excelled in business would get more benefits.

How were your expectations from the BTA fulfilled over the past 20 years?

When the negotiations were about to be wrapped up, US Ambassador to Vietnam Peterson said the BTA would help to raise Vietnam's export revenue to the US by US$6-8 billion, in which I didn't believe. I had never seen such numbers in two-way trade during my career. However, two years later, the value even exceeded the ambassador's forecast, and continued to grow further, reaching a trade surplus which Vietnam had never experienced before. The trade surplus helped to balance the country's trade with an increasing trade deficit at that time. The bilateral trade now hits nearly US$80 billion.

Despite achievements in export-import activities, there remain limitations in investment due to overlapping laws in Vietnam. More effort should be made to improve the domestic investment environment.

-What did you regret for the BTA?

I have been satisfied with the agreement. Vietnam would not have made any progress if it maintained the centrally planned economy. Thanks to the BTA, Vietnam has completed its economic transformation.

At that time, I mulled over all documents I got, reading over and over again books on US culture before the negotiations. I and my colleagues spent 5-6 years looking into each concept, as well as cultural and political characteristics of the US. We tried to find out how "civil law" was set by the US and the United Nations. During that period, we only had New Year's Eve and the first day of the Lunar New Year off. I had little time for my family. My wife was fed up with my absence at home. I rarely stayed at home although my apartment was near my office. My wife and daughters took care of themselves. I said humorously "I deserve a long holiday" following the negotiations. Since the BTA was signed, I have led a happy life. (Smile).

-Why didn't you join the WTO negotiations although you have experience?

I refused to join the negotiations for the World Trade Organization (WTO). The BTA and the WTO are different, as the trade deal was designed on the basis of the WTO, thus requiring concerned parties to understand WTO rules to put forth clauses of the BTA. For the WTO negotiations, WTO rules were automatically accepted. Negotiators for the BTA suffered huge pressure, with various legal adjustments.

For me, the tariff reduction of 1-2 percent or tariff expansion by 1-2 years would not address all problems. In the BTA negotiations, the US made many commitments. They said the US Congress would not approve such reduction as hundreds of US businesses were keeping a close watch on this matter. I said export-import tariff made up 2 percent of the US budget, while that accounted for 20 percent of Vietnam's budget. For the US, the tax revenue mainly came from asset and corporate duties and VAT. Meanwhile, there was no asset duty in Vietnam, like in my case when I owned a small apartment measuring only a few tens of sq.m, and earned hundreds of thousands of Vietnam dong each month, the amount not even enough for income tax. We had to be candid while negotiating.

With increasing mutual trust, the two sides found it easier to talk to each other later. Even after the BTA negotiations, Vietnamese and US negotiators still kept in touch. I visited their houses, had meals there and met their relatives. The WTO was formed in January 1995 when Vietnam had no idea about the organization. However, after the BTA was inked, Vietnam and US followed WTO rules. Vietnam would not reach the agreement and maintain its ties with the US if the country had no insight into the WTO.

-It is clear that thanks to the BTA, Vietnam's legal system, especially in economy, has been improved significantly. What do you think about this?

Following the BTA, the Vietnamese National Assembly issued a resolution, part of which mentioned the BTA. The legislature assigned its Standing Committee to instruct the Government to review the entire domestic legal system and compare it with commitments in the BTA. The committee was also tasked with building a law-making program in line with the BTA roadmap. The US sent experts to Vietnam. Meanwhile, the Vietnamese government asked the Ministry of Justice to coordinate with relevant ministries and agencies in the review, which found more than 170 legal documents in need of adjustments or supplements.

-It is said that WTO standards are changeable and the BTA should be re-assessed. What do you think about this?

When globalization began, the US political landscape also changed through different periods of time. President Bill

Clinton urged the formation of the WTO through the Marrakesh agreement, and encouraged local businesses to expand their operation abroad. US economic groups, therefore, optimized opportunities brought about by the globalization, and gained big profits. However, President Trump had a contrasting viewpoint: it was time for US firms to return home.

Moreover, incentives for developing countries and subsidy regulations have shown their limitations. Therefore, the setting would change in the time ahead, and the game would be redesigned to ensure fairness.

-You said when negotiating the BTA, that you stood on the line between "merit" and "crime"?

As I said, the BTA negotiations were conducted amidst the psychological impact of the war, which was understandable. It is unnecessary to identify "merit" and "crime" as I am now leading a happy life and seeking nothing for myself.

-How do you live after completing the task as the BTA chief negotiator 20 years ago?

The plowman Nguyen Dinh Luong now has a simple life. As you see, there are no valuable assets in my house. I haven't bought new furniture for many years. I have noodles and eggs for breakfast. I eat anything prepared by my children at lunch. For dinner, I have low-protein foods. I have no special demands and don't like beer and wine. I have lived on my pension. My children buy medicines for me when necessary. I plan to move to my hometown in the time ahead.

It is good as my career is not associated with money. Many people asked me to bring jeans and T-shirts home for selling when I travelled to the former Soviet Union and Eastern Europe for negotiations for 20 years, but I refused their suggestions. Although it was a trend at that time and many got rich thanks to the business, I thought that I had no capacity for it. My most valuable asset was negotiating skills and brainpower. I still keep in mind all things related to the BTA negotiations over the past 20 years.

I spent five years studying the US, so I now can spend all day talking about the country. *(Smile)*.

The 10-year BTA and unfulfilled dreams

"The legal weight of the BTA has contributed to breaking Vietnam's stagnation iceberg of the subsidized economy; toppling the copper poles supporting the ineffective "beg-give" economy."

Nguyen Dinh Luong (Vietnamnet-2011)

In retrospect, the Vietnam – U.S. BTA negotiation (Bilateral Trade Agreement) was a difficult one. It was so difficult that it makes me shiver with memory of the challenges faced 10 years ago.

On the occasion of the 10th anniversary of the BTA having been implemented, I want to share a lot, but I would like to share only 2 small stories, as unforgettable memories of the negotiation period.

The first story: Answering questions from10-year-ago

After the BTA was signed, I was the officially honored (and took responsibility) for introduction of the BTA to almost all ministries, central departments and sectors, and provinces from the north to the south in Vietnam. I have answered many questions. Specifically, there was an unanswerable one.

It was:" How could we sign the BTA at the time with such a redoubtable partner, a large-scale agreement with such complicated provisions?"

In retrospect, the same question was answered clearly by Joe Damond, Chief negotiator of the US negotiating delegation –

my esteemed counterpart, in his writing for Saigon Times Daily published early spring of 2001 that there were 3 reasons:

First, it was the endeavor made by the United States

Second, the same endeavor by Vietnam

And third, two negotiating delegations had tried their best.

I hadn't answered the question at that time, it was because I realized that it had many implications.

The questioners may have wondered what was the thinking of Vietnam side.

Today, when 10 years have gone by and I have still kept my concern, I think I have found a relatively satisfactory answer. There were 2 reasons, one was a main point and the another was secondary.

The main one playing the decisive role made by the Vietnam side was the country's demand for development.

The country needed to develop in the context of the changing world when a new race started worldwide – the rush to develop. The demand of developing the country became the national aspiration for taking off.

Vietnam is not a power. But, the Vietnamese nation is well-known for the country's highly self-strengthening independence. The 4000-year history of the nation almost saw times of being dominated and blocked by foreign powers. Our ancestors always aspire to independence and freedom.

Our independence and freedom have been paid by many generations through blood, sweat, and tears untill now. And, today's country, when evolving in the world's development, has the right and must gain the right of evolving, as a basic right of human beings.

The aspiration to develop is so strong that all social classes unanimously find it inspiring. It is strong enough to break through all obstacles though they are big or small, solid or soft. The pathway of development, as the only priority in the today's world, is integration into the world economy.

As a result, today's Vietnam is becoming more and more deeply integrated into the world economy. Vietnam has already joined ASEAN, APEC, ASEM. Also, Vietnam is a WTO member, and the country has signed or is negotiating several Free Trade Agreements (FTAs). It shows that we have chosen our pathway of going forward. The Communist Party of Vietnam has been leading the Vietnamese people forward the developing way.

What was the secondary reason?

Please looking back in history, after the Marrakesh Declaration of 15 April 1994, for the WTO establishment, the economic globalization was incited to become a vortex. Forums, workshops could be seen everywhere. Many types of agreements including financial services liberalization, or telecommunication service liberalization ones sprang up as mushrooms after rain.

Most especially, the loud start of a new round of global trade negotiations with a monumental scale - the Doha round.

The whirlwind of globalization has given non-WTO members a feeling that they must quickly join the WTO. Those missing the boat may lose opportunities and pay a higher price.

Vietnam negotiated the BTA with the United States right amongst that whirlwind and   vortex. And, the BTA is designed to be based on WTO rules, becoming a product that both Vietnam and the US have never experienced previously in all bilateral relationships. It can be said that the BTA is the unique achievement gained by a unique relationship in the no-second context. Did that give advantages or disadvantages? It would be inadequate for an evaluation because it depends on the viewpoint. So, we should temporarily suspend it.

What could be clearly acknowledged is   the hot impact of globalization's wind as well as psychological pressure.

And, particularly the legal weight of the BTA has contributed to break Vietnam's stagnating iceberg of the subsidized economy; toppled the copper poles supporting the inefficient "beg - give" economy; breaking the door bolt for the WTO wind blowing into each meeting room, hall, lecture hall, library, disassembling the legal box made of "proprietary" and "discriminatory" materials...

Then redesign a new legal framework in line with international standards, while removing obstacles in the process of implementing the Party and State's policy of mobilizing all social potential for development.

Please take a look back to the whirlwind of globalization. When it became an outbreak, the whole world rushed to run in it. Even the poor and underdeveloped countries without any awareness of it, saw the running and copied running...

After running around in circles, some calculated again to realize that they were not prepared to gain anything in this highly dynamic economic globalization. And those benefiting by globalization were mainly developed countries, or well-prepared and ready ones.

So the excitement to join waned, the wind of globalization cooled down, and the whirlwind dissipated.

As a result, without wind, the Doha boat has been now lying dormant in the harbor.

Negotiators' illusory wishes

While negotiating, both Vietnam and the US had their own targets and requirements. Vietnamese negotiators had many aspirations, including the wishes that we recognized as illusory 10 years later.

The first unfulfilled wish

We were aware that the US had the most advanced economy and was the biggest investor in the world. With firm commitments from the Vietnamese side in the BTA, especially the intellectual property program and the program on the development of the investment ties, and the Vietnamese National Assembly's amendments and supplements to the Investment Law and the Law on Intellectual Property Rights, we hoped that US investors would dominate the Vietnamese market, helping the country quickly reform its economic structure, soon escape from backwardness, join global value chains, and catch up with other countries in the region.

However, the wish has not been realized over the past decade. The US's registered capital now stands at about US$12 billion, accounting for only more than 5 percent of the total foreign investment of US$216 billion in Vietnam. Except footwear and garment-textiles, the US has yet to gain successes in the Vietnamese market.

Why?

Is it because US investors have been focusing on the Chinese market?

Actually, when Vietnam and the US missed the chance to sign the BTA in September 1999, China and the US signed an agreement on conditions for China to join the WTO later the same year, facilitating the country's joining the organization one year later. The market, with a population of 1.3 billion, had become a huge magnet to US investors and the world at large.

Is it because Vietnam could not satisfy US investors' demands, while other countries could do it?

Is it because US investors were accustomed to a transparent investment environment, and they didn't want to or couldn't surpass complex legal barriers and administrative procedures in Vietnam?

Is it because of the above-mentioned reasons or anything else?

Conclusions and causes for the issue have been established through workshops and candid dialogues. We hope that with the strong management of the Vietnamese Government, Vietnam's limitations will soon be addressed, and we continue to hope…

The second unfulfilled wish

While negotiating the BTA, I hoped that Americans would bring their business culture to Vietnam as they did in many other countries.

The US has the most dynamic economy, the most modern economic management methods and the most cutting-edge technologies.

Americans run business dynamically, effectively, scientifically, strategically and tactically.

They are also good at business administration, quality and labor management, environmental protection, marketing and maintaining productivity.

If the business culture was introduced into Vietnam, Vietnamese would optimize it and it would promote national economic development.

Over the past decade, the American business culture has yet to be found in the Vietnamese economy, even though a large number of Vietnamese have travelled to the US and another significant number of Americans have come to Vietnam, and various training classes have been held with the participation of US experts, including famous professors.

Why?

Did the US invest too little in Vietnam?

Does the psychology of a small business economy cause obstacles?

Or is it because the "Vietnamese way of doing business is like no others", as found by Virginia Foote, Chairwoman of the US-Vietnam Trade Council. Was this it also an obstacle for the American business culture" to integrate?

Maybe, all the above mentioned could be reasons , as well as others. Only one factor is that it may have taken too long time for Vietnamese to access the "American business culture" in their country.

It's good to know how beautiful and sweet flowers and fruits are, but how hard to touch.

We could haven't got the fruitful BTA and integration unless we worked much with all our might and sweat, and our blood.

But, first of all, it requires integrated thinking with deeply and fully integrated knowledge to show us how to govern the socio-economy in a period of integration.

Four tough questions from Fulbright

"In the Geneva negotiation, we had a Dien Bien Phu victory resounding throughout five continents. In the Paris negotiation, we had continuous victories on the battlefield. In the BTA negotiation, Vietnam was nothing compared to the United States."

Nguyen An Thanh

In 2000, Dr. Vu Thanh Tu Anh, who was a young and enthusiastic economic expert and trained in the United States, returned to Vietnam to teach the Fulbright program organized by the United States in Ho Chi Minh City. On the occasion of the newly-signed Vietnam-U.S BTA, he came to visit Nguyen Dinh Luong at his private home and invited Luong to talk about BTA at the school.

In July, 2020, on the occasion of the 20th anniversary of signing the Agreement, upon seeing expert Nguyen Dinh Luong on television, Dr. Vu Thanh Tu Anh, a member of the Prime Minister's economic advisory group, called Luong to invite him to lecture. With knowledgeable and enthusiastic people involved in national development like Dr. Vu Thanh Tu Anh, of course Luong accepted the invitation. Moreover, he is greatly interested in the Fulbright forum, which gathers intellectuals and elites.

However, social distancing due to the Covid-19 resurgence resulted in the online organization of the lecture from 1:30 p.m to 5:20 p.m. on August 15, 2020. The dialogue featured stories related to the BTA negotiation process, the definition of the BTA and a question-answer section. We were lucky to witness the lesson during Covid-19 time and hear Nguyen Quy Tam's good questions which were relevant to the dialogue.

Nguyen Quy Tam was Head of Interpreters and Manager of the alumni network at the Fulbright University Vietnam. He was responsible for translation at the Fulbright School of Public Policy and Management as well as coordinating the Fulbright's alumni network. He was also the main interpreter in the subjects of the Public Policy Master's Program, the senior management program and the initiative on policy dialogue.

The first question: "Can you tell us about how our delegation was organized before and during the negotiation?

Without any hesitation, expert Nguyen Dinh Luong said: "Concerning the trade field, I had attended many negotiations for nearly 20 years. Unlike the previous political negotiations such as Geneva Agreement negotiation or the Paris Agreement negotiation, in the BTA negotiation, the Government appointed the chief and required members of ministries and branches to participate. The BTA negotiation delegation had more than 40 people representing the fields of economy, science and technology, security and defense. Nevertheless, a number of key groups were formed during the preparation process:

+ Investment group

+ Intellectual property group

+ Trade and tax group

+ Group of legal issues

The groups developed plans, submitted them to the relevant ministries for "approval", transferred them to the delegation's head to assemble into a general plan, being signed by the Trade Minister, submitted them to the Prime Minister and Government for consideration and then submitted them to the seniors.

Everyone knows that although Vietnam and the United States have basically established diplomatic relations for five years, how to establish trust with partners is an art. So, what made you, a man who is supposed to be frank and able to convince a difficult partner like Joe Damond? Nguyen Quy Tam went on.

Luong, a man who has turned 81 years old, gently smiled when asked this question. He happily said "Initially, the United States didn't have trust because there were many tense issues in the Vietnam-U.S relationship. However, the trust was gradually built up through negotiation and the process of resolving its issues. According to me, to gain such trust, it's needed to have several fundamental factors, which are:

- Both sides share the same vision and work together towards a win-win agreement.

- Having in-depth understanding of issues in negotiation as well as issues raised by partners. Speakers must understand what listeners want to hear, while, listeners must comprehend what speakers want to say.

- Negotiating in an honest and frank manner. Americans like t decency and frankness.

The trust in the negotiation delegations is the trust between the two countries. That is necessary for a long-term cooperation. The U.S Chief Negotiator Joe Damond said: "We (Joe and Luong) have very different positions, but both of us share the responsibility of seeking ways to reach a mutual understanding."

Because he had closely followed the negotiation process, Tam surprised attendees at the online dialogue by his good questions on the techniques in negotiation.

-*"How did we negotiate in case we had or didn't have outstanding advantages over the partner?"*

As a well-known negotiator of the Trade Ministry, Luong said without any hesitation: "Before the BTA negotiation, I have read very carefully documents on the previous international negotiations. In the Geneva negotiation, we had a Dien Bien Phu victory resounding throughout five continents and stirring up the world. In the Paris negotiation, we had continuous victories on the battlefield, forcing the United States to withdraw. But in the BTA negotiation, we were in a completely different situation. In terms of the economy, Vietnam was nothing compared to the United States of 33/12 trillion USD. We considered:

Our advantages:

1. An independent country, respected by the world and the United States.

2. The United States also wanted to fully normalize relations with Vietnam for geopolitical purposes.

The nature of the negotiation

Perhaps, the BTA negotiation was not seeking every single piece of interest and then put it together into an Agreement. It was substantially a journey of searching and designing principles and regulations so that Vietnam's economy could connect with the United States', thereby connecting with the world's economy for development.

Results

The BTA mainly outlines what Vietnam needs to do, a roadmap it needs to supplement and a legal system it needs to amend. Basically, the United States doesn't have to do anything. So, does it mean the United States won and Vietnam lost? Does it mean that Vietnam made concession? No, I affirm that is what Vietnam must do to be able to exploit the benefits in the U.S market and then integrate into the world economy.

The online dialogue during the Covid-19 time wrapped up with a question which was not quantitative but didn't have a satisfying answer. "How did you prepare ways of designing an Agreement satisfying parties as well as achieving the desired values or at least the same degree of dissatisfaction?"

Luong was really resolute: Whether the negotiation is satisfactory depends on whether its goals are achieved. According to the flexible diplomatic motto of Ho Chi Minh, goals may be obvious from the beginning or supplemented and adjusted during the negotiation process.

For Vietnam, the first goal was finalizing the process of full normalization of relations (diplomatic ties were completed, and now it's economic ones). During the negotiation process, we discovered and added two more goals:

- To join the WTO, integrating into the world economy.

- To build a long-term business partnership with the United States.

In my opinion, we attained those three goals. We felt satisfied. The United States also showed their satisfaction through President Bill Clinton's speech and the U.S Chief Negotiator Joe Damond.

It's been a long time since I've witnessed an online dialogue satisfying both speakers and listeners. Attending the dialogue in Hanoi, I saw expert Nguyen Dinh Luong's interest in questions of Fulbright. I believed that people in Ho Chi Minh City would receive new information about the BTA negotiation process shared by insiders.

Talkshow "Vietnam- U.S Trade Agreement 25 years looking back"

From potential to comprehensive partner

"Never before has Vietnam negotiated and signed an agreement requiring such amount of adjustments and amendments of legal documents in the legal system, almost all Vietnamese economic system was touched, from trade, investment, service and intellectual property".

Anh Ngoc (Kinhte & Dothi - July 9, 2020)

The Vietnam- U.S relationship is a unique one and will continue to extensively develop in the future. This is the opinion of economic expert Nguyen Dinh Luong- Former Chief Negotiator of the Vietnam-U.S BTA at a talkshow "Vietnam- U.S Trade Agreement 25 years looking back" jointly held by Kinhtedothi Newspaper and Thuy Loi University on July 8.

BTA – a "marathon on the rope"

In retrospect the whole 5-year-long negotiation process with 11 sessions, economic expert Nguyen Dinh Luong likened the BTA to a "marathon on a tightrope" with tense and unpredictable challenges.

When the two sides began to negotiate, Vietnam's small economy still faced many difficulties after a long war, while the United States was already a giant. In 1995, Vietnam had a

GDP of 33 billion USD and an almost primitive economic law system, while the United States was very strict with laws on antitrust, anti-dumping and anti-subsidy. The underdevelopment in the Internet also restricted Vietnam in getting access to information about the U.S market.

During the process of negotiating the BTA with Vietnam, the United States first proposed talks based on WTO's standards which was a big and unfamiliar playground to Vietnam at that time.

"Never before has Vietnam negotiated and signed an agreement requiring such amount of adjustments and amendments of legal documents in the legal system, almost all the Vietnamese economic system was touched, from trade, investment, service and intellectual property," said economic expert Nguyen Dinh Luong.

The former BTA Chief Negotiator said the negotiation process sometimes fell into stalemate and faced a risk of disruption, but the BTA was finally signed on July 13, 2000 thanks to the two sides' efforts.

A wide door for Vietnamese goods

Since the BTA took effect, the United States has reduced the average tariff rate on imported goods from Vietnam to 4% from 40% and opened its doors for Vietnamese exporters. Thanks to the BTA, Vietnam's exports to the United States enjoyed vigorous growth, according to Luong. He cited: "Since the two countries normalized their relations from 1995 to 2000, Vietnam-U.S trade turnover increased to $1 billion from $450 million; but, since the enforcement of the BTA, it has boosted by an average of 20%/year. In 2019, it reached $75.7 billion, 75 times higher than that in 2000."

Notably, Vietnam's export turnover to the United States increased from $0.7 billion in 2000 to $61.3 billion in 2019. The United States' export turnover to Vietnam increased from $0.363 billion in 2000 to $14.37 billion in 2019. The United States became Vietnam's largest export market in 2019, accounting for 28.5% of the country's total export turnover. Several key items with a sharp increase including textiles and garments increased by 11.7%; footwear by 23.9%; telephones and components by 87.4%; electronics, computers and components by 35.1% compared to 2018.

A special relationship which will extensively develop in the future

Speaking on the talk show, economic expert Nguyen Dinh Luong affirmed that the Vietnam - US relationship was a special one. That was because from sworn enemies, the two countries had become partners which have complemented each other and taken the economy as the center. "The BTA is an important premise for the economy as well as other international relations to develop. Thanks to the rapid development of economic relations, the Vietnam-U.S relationship has been deepened. It can be said that the BTA has pushed the Vietnam-U.S relations to another level, putting the economy at the center," Luong commented.

Vietnam and the Unites States have made a significant progress in normalizing and beefing up their diplomatic relations during the past 25 years. The obvious manifestation for the development of this special relationship is that despite the difficult time, the two countries have effectively cooperated and made great strides.

Luong took the example that amid the rampant Covid-19 situation, the U.S Department of State on March 27, 2020 announced a package of 274 million USD in humanitarian and emergency health assistance to 64 countries including Vietnam to help them in their Covid-19 fight.

The former BTA Chief Negotiator also forecast that Vietnam-U.S relations would continue to extensively develop. The United States has foreseen Vietnam's important strategic position in Southeast Asia. Vietnam currently acquires a high prestige in ASEAN.

Two stories about the Negotiator

From public affairs to sidewalk fruit vendor

"The international economic integration is intensive and helps Vietnam's economy develop, but it hasn't yet brought the country out of the middle-income trap."

Linh Anh-Hoang Ly (CafeF.vn - 2020)

Taking the entrance exam to Hanoi University of Science and Technology with a dream of becoming a mechanical engineer, Luong was suddenly sent to the Soviet Union to study "foreign trade", a major which was so strange at that time that students jokingly called it "treating the skin diseases."

A "rustic" student with a predestined relationship in negotiations

Graduating from high school, Nguyen Dinh Luong took the entrance exam to Hanoi University of Science and Technology with the dream of becoming an engineer who can manufacture machines for his hometown. One month after the admission, Nguyen Dinh Luong was informed by his Dean that he was being sent to the Soviet Union to study. After the basic Russian course at Gia Lam University of Foreign Languages, Hanoi, the student at the machine-manufacturing faculty departed to study foreign trade at the Moscow State Institute of International Relations.

At that time, very few people understood what "foreign trade" was, so, when asking, the student at the machine-manufacturing faculty was told that "foreign trade may be treating skin diseases." Nowadays, everyone can affirm that is a joke. However, 60 years ago, perhaps those saying that really didn't know, instead of joking.

In fact, when dividing majors to study in the Soviet Union, the "hot" majors included maths, physics, philosophy, electricity and medicine, while, foreign trade was just a "stepchild". Knowing his major was foreign trade, the "rural" student thought that it was "a limitation of his fate".

"I'm from the countryside and not supported by anyone. I had to do whatever assigned by the organization and didn't dare to complain. I understood the limitations in my life and that the only way to rise was to study better," said Nguyen Dinh Luong.

Nevertheless, during the time studying in Moscow, Nguyen Dinh Luong discovered that his school was a place to train children of senior diplomatic leaders of Eastern European countries. Many graduates from this school became international negotiators and the Vietnamese student began to nurture a new dream.

He cherished the dream of becoming an international negotiator, but when returning home, Nguyen Dinh Luong was tasked to teach at the Foreign Trade University. Here, he strove to become the Secretary of the school union of a typical school of the Central Youth Union. He then joined the Party and became the head of the Personnel and Organization

Department, the Organization Board and the Party Inspection Commission.

In 1978, Luong was suddenly asked to move to Department 1 under the Trade Ministry (in charge of the socialist countries). At that time, Vietnam was preparing negotiation to join SEV (the Council for Mutual Economic Assistance- Socialist), so, the Trade Ministry really needed experts majoring in foreign affairs and trade as well as being good at Russian. This was a turning point in Nguyen Dinh Luong's career.

Working as a generalist in Department 1 for a short time, Luong was sent to the Soviet Union to study economic management within one year. Luong then went to work right after returning home. He was assigned to prepare documents to work with the Hungarian delegation. Because the department's leader went on the overseas business trip, Luong became the representative of Department 1's leader to work with the Hungarian delegation with the title of " Deputy Director General." "The decision to appoint Luong as deputy director was discussed and agreed by the ministry's leadership but hadn't been transformed into a document because the minister was on the business trip," a deputy minister said.

Over the next 10 years since then, Luong had had the opportunity to negotiate and make friends with "leaders in many fraternal socialist countries". Negotiator Nguyen Dinh Luong has traveled to many socialist countries all over the world. Every quarter, he attended the SEV meetings in Moscow; every year, he visited countries such as North Korea, Cuba and Albania. He even stayed in Moscow for more than 3 months.

During those years, Luong established intimate friendships which helped him to handle smoothly in the negotiation of debt repayment of socialist countries in the 1980s and early 1990s.

In the late 1980s, when Eastern European countries faced difficulties, they started to collect debts from Vietnam. In 1989, the Soviet Union also began to do that.

"They demanded to be paid back in coffee and rubber, while we had little. Everyone and I had to research and sought ways to repay debts appropriately," said Luong. Polish people liked giving simple gifts to each other on holidays and birthdays, thus, the Vietnamese negotiation delegation successfully proposed to repay the debts with sedge baskets and handicrafts. With Romania, Vietnam settled the debts with broken coal (Romania has a metallurgical industry, so, it was in need of coal). With Russia, 1 million liters of new rice volka wine and 1 million square meters of jute carpet were used to pay off debts."

Not only did they help Vietnam clear its debts and satisfy its partners, but these agreements were also very useful to the Vietnamese people. Jute farmers in Thai Binh and Nam Dinh were very happy. Wine factories mushroomed and the main materials for production were cassava and corn.

After many years of negotiating agreements with socialist countries, Luong became the Director of Department 1 and continued his work with capitalist nations such as Singapore, Canada and a number of non-EU countries like Norway and Switzerland.

The Agreement of a lifetime and origins of the "United States' conspiracy"

In the 1990s, at the Trade Ministry, Nguyen Dinh Luong was a leader with the most experience in negotiating international trade agreements. When appointed as the Chief Negotiator at the Vietnam-U.S BTA, Luong considered it as his "Agreement of a lifetime." The BTA is Vietnam's first big international trade one but the last for Luong as the Chief Negotiator.

When the BTA negotiation was kicked off, Vietnam-US relationships were briefly described by two words "former foes": the United States was the loser in the war, but Vietnam also suffered great losses and pain. The trust between the two sides stood at a low level. In Vietnam, the words of former US Secretary of State Henry Kissinger have haunted many people, especially these important ones: "If we can't win Vietnam in war, we must win it in peace". That's reason why many people consider the BTA a "United States' conspiracy".

In fact, apart from the lack of trust with the United States, the awareness of international economic integration or globalization in Vietnam at that time was also at the same level. Nguyen Dinh Luong still vividly remembers the speech of a leader at a scientific conference themed "Globalization and its effects on Vietnam" as saying:

"Globalization is the game of the bourgeoisie, it only causes poverty and a wider gap between the rich and poor. We need to wait for globalization led by the proletariat."

Luong still remembers his additional argument after giving many analyses on the impacts of globalization on Vietnam: "How long do we have to wait for the globalization led by proletariat? In which countries in the world will the proletariat implement globalization?

Therefore, when becoming the Chief Negotiator at the BTA, Luong understood that he not only had to negotiate with the United States but also had to convince the Vietnamese people to believe in the benefits brought by the agreement. The Chief Negotiator's duties included not only the terms agreed in the BTA, but also how to get domestic consensus on the agreement.

During the process of seeking domestic support for the signing of the BTA, Luong many times felt hurt. At a workshop on the BTA, Luong expressed his opinion about President Bill Clinton: "In the history of Vietnam-U.S relations, there hasn't been any president treating Vietnam better than Bill Clinton," and then gave examples. Luong immediately received the comment: "It is an ambiguous class position. How can the power of imperialism can treat Vietnam well?".

Integration story and the sidewalk of the BTA Chief Negotiator's house

After the BTA was signed, Luong gave an impressive interview about his delight: "It's like a farmer finishing plowing a field, smoking a tobacco pipe, and releasing smoke into the sky. So ecstatic!".

Behind the joy of a negotiator who had completed his task, Luong had another pride that could not be expressed: "The BTA offers opportunities for Vietnam to integrate into the global economy. The economic integration will force changes to the old thinking and next generations will no longer suffer poverty as we did. In fact, the BTA opens new doors for Vietnam's economy to develop: new, more progressive laws are enacted, business gets more new opportunities, and the subsidized and planning mechanism are wiped out".

After the landmark changes from BTA, Vietnam negotiated to join the WTO and many other free trade agreements. The economy has enjoyed a variety of benefits from integration. Particularly, the US-Vietnam trade ties have gained outstanding achievements which even surprised insiders.

When the two countries normalized their relations in 1995, the Vietnam - US trade turnover rose from $450 million to $1.09 billion in 2000. However, since the signing of the BTA, trade turnover has increased by an average of 20%/year. In 2019, it reached $75.72 billion, 75 times higher than that in 2000."

Vietnam's export turnover to the United States in 2000 stood at $0.733 billion and increased to $14.37 billion in 2019. Last year, the United States became Vietnam's largest export market, occupying 28.5% of the country's total export turnover. The American Chamber of Commerce in Vietnam (AmCham) said that Vietnam had increasingly enhanced its position as the US's leading supplier in the ASEAN region.

For many years, there has been a fresh fruit street vendor in front of Luong's house which is hardly seen in front of other houses on Dang Tien Dong street (Hanoi).

The vendor's female owner said "He allows me to sit here and my fruit is placed at his house when the ward authorities clear the sidewalk. I'm so lucky to have a free area on the sidewalk to sell fruit.

The image of the fruit street vendor is probably not what Luong expected to see in the changes to Vietnam after 20 years of BTA implementation. However, it reflects an undeniable fact: The international economic integration is intensive and helps Vietnam's economy develop, but it hasn't yet brought the country out of the middle-income trap.

As well as accepting missing previous opportunities in negotiation, the BTA Chief Negotiator Nguyen Dinh Luong sympathizes with the vendor in front of his house.

"Her name is Ly, from Ha Dong. She has been selling fruit in front of my house for a long time to support her mother and children. The rice cooker of her whole family lies there. Her children's tuition fee lies there. Having a stable area for selling fruit, her life has been less difficult, especially during pandemic time," Luong said

However, permitting Ly to sell fruit in front of his house stems from the sympathy of a person born in an agricultural family as a manual worker.

"My mother in my hometown worked even more strenuously than her. Therefore, I permit such strenuous people to sit in front of my house to sell goods without paying any fee. Earning a little money can raise children," said Nguyen Dinh Luong.

PART 3

ECONOMIC INTEGRATION VIEWED BY THE EXPERT NEGOTIATOR

How the BTA and the WTO accession process affect Vietnam's economy

"It should cut down movements, eliminate races for credit mania. It's high time to spend time, effort, and knowledge finding different ways of following the rules to help our country to avoid lagging far behind, and prevent our nation from continuously being harmed due to an inferiority complex to other nations."

Nguyen Dinh Luong

Speaking at the workshop:" Vietnam's economy – Opportunities and Challenges, Impact of the global financial crisis" held at the Majestic hotel, Ho Chi Minh city on September, 9, 2010.

The topics of the WTO and BTA's impact on the Vietnamese economy have been discussed continuously on mass media and at many forums in Vietnam. Of course, it seemed that opinions have always varied.

The WTO and BTA were said to create successes for the state-owned economic sectors, but integration was also considered as the cause of difficulties faced by the economy. In general, the major issues to address still haven't been settled. So, the discussions on that may last for long time.

Why then should we and recall the commitments we made in to the BTA and discuss the WTO before controversies arise over their impact?

1. International commitments (BTA and WTO) are just meant to build a better legal framework regulating our economy and to open the Vietnamese market to integrating into the world economy.

Both the Vietnam – US bilateral trade agreement (BTA) and the WTO accession process aim to deal with 2 issues, and put in legal terms, there are two commitments:

+ Building and improving the Vietnamese legal system in accordance with international rules.

+ Opening the market, opening the Vietnamese economy for its integration into the world economy.

Though the contents are the same, they are different in terms of methods and scale of commitment.

* ***On legal framework***

- Vietnam, in negotiating the BTA, just began the country's measures toward integrating into the international economy while still operating the economy in its own way with the goal of "building an independent and self-reliant economy".

The BTA negotiation was to design a legal framework regulating all economic and trade activities between Vietnam and the Unites States. The legal framework is designed based on WTO standards and regulations which were considered to be quite new to Vietnam's socialist legal system that time, especially to several basic principles such as open and transparent law, equality and non-discrimination between domestic and imported goods, between national and international enterprises..etc.

Those international regulations were inevitably going to "collide" with the current legal framework of Vietnam at that time, and moreover, they almost required a complete "refresh" of our legal system in order to be accordance with international law.

Our Government, to fulfill the commitments in the BTA, implemented a "general review" of the legal system in 2001, compared it with the provisions of the BTA and the WTO, and designed a program to develop legislation submitted to the National Assembly. The National Assembly of the 2001-2005 tenure has supplemented and renewed most of the laws and basic laws regulating our country's economy and society.

- The WTO negotiation, differing from the BTA negotiation, follows its own process. Moreover, Vietnam and WTO did not conduct a negotiation of building a legal framework, because Vietnam was supposed to automatically accept and comply with all WTO regulations when joining the WTO.

Thus, the only discussible issue was reviewing all the laws of Vietnam to amend those which were contrary to the WTO. Therefore, the WTO negotiation was essentially a general international review, chaired by the WTO, the entire Vietnam's legal system, from legal documents to law enforcement. Basing on this review, the "Documents of Vietnam's accession to the WTO" was formed, which clearly stated which laws Vietnam committed to supplement and adjust and how to correct them....

Thus, the BTA and WTO negotiations can be considered as a two-stage process in which Vietnam gradually built an open, transparent and non-discriminatory legal system to integrate into the world economy

- *On commitments of opening the market*

- The additional and amended law itself was our way to open the market and the half – open economy at that time.

- The market opening also commits to removing all non-tariff barriers, invalid protection measures, to reduce tariffs, and open the market for all kinds of services according to the roadmap.

- Regarding tariffs, in the BTA, we had only committed to reducing more than 200 tax lines, because at that time we had not reformed our tax system, so much reduction would affect budget revenue. In the WTO, we committed to the entire tariff schedule and reducing more taxes according to a schedule as same as other countries which have joined the WTO.

- Regarding the services market in the WTO, we made more commitments but basically stayed the same with the BTA on the level of openness.

- In the BTA, the investment field contains more commitments, and is broader and tighter to form a legal framework regulating the investment field between Vietnam and the United States. In the WTO, there are only provisions on "Trade-Related Investment Measures".

- Therefore, commitments in the BTA and WTO are a roadmap to open the economy and the Vietnamese market in investment, trade and services.

Today, the Vietnamese market has become one of the emerging open markets.

As the legal system has been simplified and the domestic market has expanded, Vietnam has been potentially affected by both positive and negative aspects of the world market. When the world economy is in peak season, it also brings fruitful results to Vietnam and the Vietnamese economy will have a chance to grow. On the other hand, when the world economy is in crisis and collapses, Vietnam's economy also follows this slowdown.

After the BTA and WTO, Vietnam's economy had the opportunity to develop well and quickly, but when the world faced a financial crisis, the Vietnamese economy also suffered much. Thanks to the Government's good sailing of the national boat, today we are considered to be temporarily "out of danger".

2. The new legal framework and market opening are only necessary conditions for economic development, but the investment increase is conditional upon others which a national strategy on socio-economy has to be given top priority.

Almost all worldwide nations are already WTO members. The WTO's legal framework and its legal system have been matched, markets and economies have also opened, but the fact is that not every country's economy developed well. The reason is the country's internal factors, the first being the superstructure including the national development policy and strategy.

The current world economy is a globalized one which mutually connects and links, and also competes and is interdependent. The country which successfully determines its position in the global system and realizes the methods and the points of connecting in order to for take advantage for itself will create its breakthrough opportunity.

In that context of globalization, it is difficult for underdeveloped and developing countries including Vietnam, with products obtained just from available resources to grow the economy, instead basing growth on developing process, assembly, employment, sales agents for developed countries and multinational corporations. They have the capital and technology to dominate production and global supply chains as well as the consumption market and demand.

Though Vietnamese is proud of its rich resources, those resources will be under the ground forever unless they use the money and technology of these parties to exploit it. Though we think that our labor force is abundant, the manpower will be unemployed without their money, machines and equipment for produding goods.

After researching, surveying, and calculating, regions and countries are considered for suitable production of which components and accessories made by what kinds of factories and where to set up the whole assembly for finished products...with quantity, quality , packaging, design, market... all decided by the big bosses.

Our enterprises have been growing rapidly and reaching about half a million companies at this time. They are struggling. Most of them are small-sized businesses whose greatest part is very small-sized with little capital, low business management skills and without a capability for operating large-scale production and real competitive advantage in the international market. The great many of them, if doing business in the field of industries or services, were struggling to seek contracts of assembly, processing, manufacturing, and sales agents for foreign owners. They can only afford to survive sustainably while struggling with increasingly fierce competition without reaching the national and international level to have strategies connecting them in the globalized economy. They still have to expect many things from the State.

Review routes mapped out for the FDI entering Vietnam

- When Vietnam started to open, it legally allowed foreign companies, after researching and surveying, to invest in building factories (simple construction), moving accessories and components from abroad into Vietnam, employing locally intensive labors, quickly assembling what in Vietnam was scarce in but highly demanded such as: motorbikes, fridges, TVs, etc, or joint-venturing with Vietnam to organize production of bricks, tiles, ceament, roofing sheets…etc.

Those all were to "serve" Vietnam. When the demand on that household goods market was relatively met, and Vietnamese people were a little better off, they began to put emphasis into assembling more advanced things to "serve" such as: large LCD TVs, multi-functional refrigerators, multi-speed washing machines, cars of all kinds, etc. Moreover, the industry was further promoted through manufacturing some accessories, spare parts for domestic market or export to complete products such as lights, electronic components, etc.

- When the Internet and IT entered Vietnam, their demands were quickly met by deployment of sales agents, and components imported into computer assembly organizations.

- When Vietnam prepared to open its market to EU and the US, surveys of selecting outsourcing partners were quickly implemented, in addition to organizing 100% foreign capital companies to produce garments, footwear products as soon as possible for export to the large markets of EU, America.

- As Vietnamese law became more open with the WTO accession, many richer social classes were formed; and they invested in real estate, building high-class apartments for sale, and luxury resorts…

- Currently, foreign investors are waiting for the development of a high-quality Vietnamese technical labor force, and when the law of intellectual property rights protection is better implemented, they will organize more accessories and spare part outsourcing for higher-tech products. Intel Corporation is making an effort to do this..

It can be seen that foreign investors in Vietnam do business methodically based on surveys, doing research, followed by cautious steps sometimes fast, sometimes slow depending on the time and invested products.

While the Vietnamese market was realized without any lens, it has showed its potential clearly, what can be exploited, how much and when.

Vietnam's economic development strategy?

Internally in Vietnam, have we also developed strategies and routes to guide both domestic and foreign-invested enterprises, to put us on the right path to lead our country's economy into the value chains which take shape in the world economy?

We have prepared all kinds of strategies and plans: 5 year, 10 year, 20 year ones but it is far different to turn those into real life. Our strategy is mainly a full expression of will, aspiration and desire.

3. The international commitments (BTA and WTO) don't include content guiding countries how to conduct their internal economic management.

While foreign investors find Vietnam's potential for doing business, they will not spend their time and capital on Vietnam without sufficient profit or less profit than other destinations.

Foreign investors (and also domestic) are of many types, including large, medium and small sizes. Many of them are true investors, doing business methodically with a desire to build a long-term platform here, needing a public and transparent investment environment for a methodical approach to the evaluation of their investment. On the other hand, there are types of investment that only aim to "seize some benefit", reap benefit in a beneficial environment to fish in troubled water.

Foreign investors enterVietnam with all kinds of business cultures. Many companies bring source or standard technology while some bring refurbished, discarded items to enter. There are businesses paying Vietnamese workers 100-150 million dong per month, having Saturday and Sunday as rest days to regenerate the labor force. Whilst, also some garment and shoe factories pay workers around 1 million dong per month but force them to work 12-14 hours/day, even on Saturdays and Sundays without payment, and cheat on their salary and insurance as well as beating workers. Beside factories strictly implementing labor laws and environmental laws, there are also some secretly dumping toxic wastewater to pollute rivers.

And so is the integration and market opening, with entering has both positive and negative effects.

However, the positive ones will expand and negative ones be eliminated if the host is wise, well-organized and conducts a methodical operation.

Virginia Foote, Board President of the US-Vietnam Trade Council, who has always been concerned and made many contributions to the normalization of political and economic relations between the US and Vietnam, and struggled with the Vietnamese market for more than 20 years had this to say: "Vietnam's way of doing business is like none other".

The world's societies are being managed and the economies are run according to the law, all society's members live and work following legal regulations. Enterprises must follow the law to do business, and management agencies strictly follow the law to supervise, inspect and handle violations.

In Vietnam, though the legal system is adequate enough, few people study it carefully to understand it until they are facing legal charges. After decentralization, the direction and guidance from the top are rarely available or unspecific, while the local authorities have no comprehensive information, thus usually discuss in teams and take a decision subject to the majority of votes.

The most recent has been seen the collapse of Vinashin group, which borrowed billions of dollars from abroad and poured money down the drain. The group made 86,000 billion dong (equal to $6 billion) evaporate but eleven inspection teams came and still praised its good operation. In fact the story looked like a fake one. How can Vietnam revive if the country had a few more companies like Vinashin? The Vedan Company after 14 years of toxic discharge, were guilty of polluting a river without anyone paying attention, until people on the riverbanks could no longer live with the pollution, before the press got involved. That woes of managing and doing business is making true investors worried. We will continuously pay the price unless we change our way of doing business.

It should cut down movements, eliminate races for credit mania. It's high time to spend time, effort, knowledge to find different ways of following rules to help our country avoid lagging far behind, preventing our nation from continuously being harmed due to an inferiority complex to other nations.

While we affirm our achievements in economic development in general and in investment in particular in the past few decades as being great, but we are not complacent about our achievements; by the identification of inadequacies, the things that have not been recognized, then we can do better, which is also a matter of discussion.

The United States is owned by Americans

"Looking back at its history, the US has never been seen to ask for any membership submission. The country would seek coordination to form a new organization when needed."

Nguyen Minh Duc

The US has witnessed chaos after the Presidential election. Incumbent President Donald Trump has refused to concede the election and is trying to overturn it.

Trump believes that he must win the election, and spend another four years in office.

Joe Biden, a Democratic presidential nominee who served as Barack Obama's Vice President, also believes in his win. Local media recognizes Biden as the president-elect. Many countries have extended congratulations to him. The man has begun his Cabinet picks.

Q: *As a former negotiator with the US for many years, what do you think about this?*

Nguyen Dinh Luong: The United States is composed of Americans. Whoever gets more electoral voters will become US President. If Trump fails to reach 270 electoral votes, he will not win the election even when he files election lawsuits or makes other efforts.

Q: *If Joe Biden becomes the US President, how will economic and trade ties between the US and other countries change, as compared with those under Trump's administration?*

Nguyen Dinh Luong: Donald Trump's Republican Party and Joe Biden's Democratic Party would differ in leadership, but they share the goal of making the US maintain its leadership and domination in the world economy.

The US and Americans have always been always proud of their legal system, which is considered the most adequate and stable for a market economy and a model for the world. The US and Americans have formed and led such economic organizations as GATT47, GATT94, WTO, APEC and TPP whose rules are copies of the US law.

Although there are certain differences between Trump and Biden, as well as the Republican and Democratic Parties, the US policies remain a systematic and consistent goal. Therefore, changes would not be made in one day. The US will continue to set rules based on their economic and military strength to lead and dominate the world.

Once becoming the US President, Biden will have to make some changes as he had committed to during his run for office. On the other hand, he will need to accept and inherit certain legacies whether he likes them or not. Observers said Trump used his last days to lock in policies not only in trade but also in military and foreign affairs. His move would be a fait accompli by the time Biden is sworn in.

Q: *Does the US want to reform or withdraw from WTO?*

Nguyen Dinh Luong: The US gave birth to the World Trade Organization (WTO) from the General Agreement on Tariffs and Trade (GATT). The WTO has been scaled up, covering almost the whole world. There are countries that have violated their commitments in intellectual property and corporate subsidy, leading to "an imbalance in interests" and making WTO lose its discipline.

Americans are interested in and will coordinate with a number of other countries to re-organize or revamp the WTO to create common rules for the world.

Q: *Many said Joe Biden will return the US to the Trans-Pacific Partnership (TPP) or the Comprehensive and Progressive Agreement for Trans-Pacific Partnership (CPTPP). Some even held that the US will re-sign a comprehensive agreement with Vietnam to replace the US-Vietnam Bilateral Trade (BTA). What do you think about these opinions?*

Nguyen Dinh Luong: Right after taking office, Donald Trump withdrew the US from the TPP following its signing.

The remaining member countries formed the CPTPP without the US. The deal, however, "suspended" about 20 provisions initiated by the US, including those on investment agreement and grants, the settlement of telecom disputes, the minimum standard of treatment, bidding procedures, nation treatment, patent term extension and relevant rights, and intellectual property protection, among others.

The move demonstrates the remaining countries' wish for the US return as the US serves as the locomotive (making up 62 percent of the TPP's GDP) and plays the leading role in an international economic organization. However, Joe Biden has yet to make any statement about this. Looking back at history, the US has never had to ask for a membership in an organization. The country would seek coordination to form a new organization when needed.

The Vietnam-US relationship has developed fruitfully in the principle of mutual respect, no matter who is the President.

Vietnam's geo-political advantages and policy of harmony have also facilitated such relations.

By Nguyen An Thanh

Playing the same "game on the WTO playing field" to know who you are

The WTO is now gathering up to 147 member countries across the world. Is Vietnam "brave" enough to be a "lonely knight", separating from the world?

Viet Lam (Vietnamnet, March 31, 2004)

Vietnam's efforts paid off as the BTA was signed after five years of negotiations. Two years after the deal came into force, Vietnam's export to the US hit 4 billion USD, accounting for one fifth of the Southeast Asian nation's total export value. The BTA also created a foundation for Vietnam to join WTO. Nguyen Dinh Luong, former Assistant to the Minister of Trade and Chief Negotiator for the BTA, is one of the people who laid the foundation.

Our conversation was about issues regarding Vietnam's economic integration, starting from a simple philosophy: "The plowman must look ahead to create straight furrows…"

Q: *"Integration" has been viewed as a 'trend". As a person who greatly contributed to the country's economic integration, what do you think about economic integration?*

Nguyen Dinh Luong: I have kept a close watch on economic integration programs and looked into relevant documents. But all of them have failed to mention the most core issue – What is economic integration?

There may be different definitions of economic integration. It can be understood as follows:

-First, from the perspective of economic movement, economic integration means connecting a national economy with the world economy, making the national economy become part of the world economy and the national market become part of the world market.

The world economy always evolves and changes. In the era when economic globalization is a natural trend, countries should connect their economies with the world economy to move ahead. In fact, the Vietnamese economy has been closely linked with the world economy. A range of economic sectors require foreign investors to further develop.

Second, from the perspective of economic and trade policies, only through economic and market opening, Vietnam would address its shortage of resources such as capital, technology and management knowledge. With the new resources, and its available resources (workforce and natural resources), the country would bring into full play its economic potential to move ahead. Vietnam opens doors for other countries to exploit its potential. Once it grows stronger, Vietnam can utilize the potential of the world market.

Market opening means gradually removing barriers like regulations on trade licenses and quota, and other regulations that run counter to international investment rules regarding the balance of export-import and foreign exchange, localization, and prices of electricity, water and transport and telecom services, while cutting import tariffs considered high as compared with the region and the world at large.

Third, from the organization perspective or joining regional and international economic organizations, including the ASEAN Free Trade Area (AFTA), the Asia-Pacific Economic Cooperation (APEC) and WTO.

WTO is now bringing together 147 countries, including the richest like the US, the largest like China, and the poorest and smallest nations. Vietnam filed a dossier to join the organization on January 3, 1995 but has yet to be admitted.

Fourth, from the legal perspective, the world is targeting a common legal framework in the economic sector. It is the framework of the WTO, which has regulated the trading of goods and services, intellectual property rights, and part of the investment sector. The framework is being supplemented and perfected through negotiations. Although it is not perfect yet, the framework is too massive and new for Vietnam, requiring the country to create a legal ground. Meanwhile, for a long time, investors in Vietnam have operated in line with the Investment Law, State-owned enterprises have observed the Law on State-owned Enterprises and private firms have followed the Business Law. There are overlapping and inconsistent regulations in the domestic laws. The State has recently assigned the Ministry of Planning and Investment to develop a Business Code and an Investment Code, which is a rosy sign.

Q: *We have seen integration as an objective need for economic development, which requires many factors to be successful?*

Nguyen Dinh Luong: Because economic integration is participating in the world economy that operates on the principle of free competition. To be successful in integration, Vietnam needs to build a competitive economy. If Vietnam fails to compete with other countries, it's economy will lose, and it will become a "second banana."

Competitiveness of an economy is formed by such factors as:

+ An economic structure adaptable to the economic structure of the modern world (Vietnam's economic structure remains backward as compared with the world's, with 76 percent of its population living on agriculture).

+ Advanced macroeconomic policies and economic management methods that match the market, modern economy (as long as the State is used to giving and businesses are used to waiting for distributions, there will not be a competitive economy).

+ Competitiveness of the economic sector, businesses and goods (technology, and quality and price management).

Q: *Many people said Vietnam's core task in anticipation of the WTO membership, or economic integration, is to identify goods of where it is highly competitiveness, in which to make investments? What do you think about the view?*

- To some extent, this view is persuasive. However, I think that building a competitive economy by identifying competitive products as Vietnam is doing is just taking into account static factors. Meanwhile, we all know the world economy always changes and evolves. Garment-textiles is an example. In the 19th century, the UK was seen as the world's garment centre, which was then moved to Europe. In the 20th century, the position was taken over by Japan, and it is assumed by China, India and Vietnam at present. The centre will gradually be shifted to less developed countries. The industry has constantly evolved and only stopped in a country as long as workers' wage remains low. When will Vietnam lose the position? It requires efforts of strategists. Moreover, Vietnam's export structure remains backward. In 2000, for example, agro-fishery products accounted for up to 60 percent of the country's exports. Among the remaining 40 percent, products from labor-intensive industries made up the majority.

-Among the above-said factors, what does Vietnam already have?

-Documents adopted at the ninth National Party Congress fully mention the issue. In implementing Party resolutions, the Politburo issued Resolution No. 07 dated November 27, 2001 on international economic integration. In implementing the Politburo's Resolution No. 07, the Prime Minister issued Decision No. 37/2002/QD-TTg dated March 14, 2002 on the US-Vietnam Bilateral Trade Agreement. These documents clearly prescribe targets, tasks and deadlines. They, however, have yet to be realized.

Q: *Businesses will play the main role in economic integration and penetration into the world market. In the past, Vietnamese enterprises have made great efforts, but they met a range of difficulties. Which support do they need to integrate into the world successfully?*

-To help business integrate successfully and grow stronger in the domestic and international market, it requires:

+A strong government that can regulate the market economy smoothly

+A strong legal system

+A strong arbitration system

+A network of strong legal assistance agencies (bar association, notary and valuation services)

+A good law information system

+A contingent of well-trained legal and judicial experts (including those in State-owned agencies and consulting organizations).

Q: *Vietnam has joined AFTA and APEC, and is seeking the WTO membership. Many are afraid that after joining the organization, Vietnamese goods will be unable to compete with imports and Vietnam will never build a self-reliant industry. Some said even developed countries have also shown a tendency of trade protectionism?*

+It is necessary to accurately understand challenges and opportunities generated by the WTO. Countries worldwide are sharing an economic playing field. ground. Integration means joining them on the playground. The process enables Vietnam to acknowledge its capacity and the effectiveness of ongoing rules, and learn from other countries' experience to grow together. Opportunities and challenges come from economic and market opening, and the common playground.

The organization has now gatherered up to 147 countries across the world. Is Vietnam "brave" enough to be a "lonely knight", separating from the world?

And how will the world talk about Vietnam – a country discussing integration a lot but failing to enter the WTO.

The view on developed countries' tending to beef up trade protection policies is wrong. In fact, they always strongly back trade liberalization that benefits them.

-Q: *Apart from the WTO, countries worldwide are seeking to reach free trade agreements (FTA). Many questioned why Vietnam has not signed FTAs with other countries.*

+FTAs have become popular in the world. The US has signed deals with Chile, Jordan and Mexico. Singapore and Australia have also reached agreements with the US. This is an inevitable phenomenon as the WTO is shared by the world, and once the organization is too small, countries have to seek their own ways to develop, especially amidst the failure on the Doha round.

Before asking whether Vietnam can engage in FTAs or not, it is a must to understand their nature. Based on FTAs signed by countries, it can be said that FTAs are WTO+. They are the expansion of the WTO on the basis of the organization's rules. The expansion, however, depends on the economic development and structure of signatories. Competition requires the removal of monopoly and the building of a legal system that gives no room to monopoly. Investment registration and grant must be carried out publicly in line with regulations. The answer is sure to be clear.

Success will not come if you make no changes

"I don't think that the US will withdraw from WTO. It only requires a stronger revamp in the organization, which must be conducted by the US."

Nguyen Dinh Luong (Dau Thau [Bidding] newspaper – 2019)

The integration playground has seen dramatic changes. Notably, WTO is in need of a strong reform. Meanwhile, many countries, including Vietnam has engaged in new-generation free trade agreements (FTAs).

Nguyen Dinh Luong, Vietnam's former Chief Negotiator for the US-Vietnam Bilateral Trade Agreement (BTA) granted an interview to the Dau Thau (Bidding) newspaper regarding the situation and trends of global trade, as well as requirements for Vietnam during the implementation of the new-generation FTAs.

Who has set the rules?

The US President on August 13 announced that the country will withdraw from WTO if there is no progress. This was not the first time President Trump warned of the withdrawal. He repeatedly said the US has been treated unequally in international trade, so Washington should not observe all of the WTO rules. Trump also held that WTO must reform its operation.

What is the WTO? It is an organization gathering 164 economies worldwide. It is also a legal framework operating the globalized economy based on three principles – free trade, open economy, transparent and fair economic environment with no discrimination.

WTO's legal framework is the inevitable result of globalization, which has led to the next period of development with the formation of various new-generation FTAs. Such deals as the Comprehensive and Progressive Agreement for Trans-Pacific Partnership (CPTPP) or the EU-Vietnam Free Trade Agreement (EVFTA) have been formed on the basis of other FTAs between the US and other countries. In other words, the US has set the rules of the game, and globalization is the internationalization of its legal system. Notably, the new-generation FTAs have entered a higher level as compared with WTO commitments. CPTPP and EVFTA have prompted member countries to change their economic management methods, not just tariff reduction.

Trend of breaking the rules

The globalization is taking place with noted changes in various aspects. Countries worldwide, rich or poor, want to grow as quickly as possible. New political trends are being formed in the evolving world.

Unlike previous US Presidents who worked to promote globalization, Trump pursued the motto of "America First." Many countries and a number of organizations, therefore, feel that they cannot fully rely on the US, and have to gradually build up their own forces, leading to the development of opportunism.

Moreover, after more than two decades of formation and development, the WTO has begun to reveal limitations like inequality and countries failing to realize their commitments. WTO prohibits copyright infringement, and export and state-owned enterprise subsidies, which, however, remain popular in many countries. The organization has also shown lax management, unserious observation of law and unclear reward and punishment mechanisms.

Notably, the US believes that it faces disadvantages in many aspects as many developed countries still maintain their "developing status" to enjoy incentives. President Trump, therefore, has moved to break WTO rules, including its decision to raise tariffs on Chinese goods. The US said the imposition of these tariff sanctions is not based on WTO rules but US legal regulations.

If this happens, the WTO legal framework would be broken. Global value chains would then be disrupted as they are operating in line with WTO rules and have their centres based on major economic groups, mostly from the US. Once the value chains are disrupted, the world economy might step back to protectionism.

I don't think that the US will withdraw from the WTO. It only requires a stronger revamp in the organization, which targets more equality and effectiveness, and the operation of the reward and punishment mechanisms. The reform must be conducted by the US. The negotiation is expected to get tough and takes time.

Adaptation and change

With the new mindset, Vietnam should be well aware of its position in the flow of economic globalization.

Vietnam needs to adapt to changes in WTO, while making efforts to satisfy and materialize standards set at EVFTA and CPTPP.

EVFTA and CPTPP are not only the deals aiming to open up the market but also a common legal framework operating member economies and a legal corridor regulating their economic links.

Joining new-generation FTAs give a new boost to market and investment activities. More importantly, their regulations and commitments have prompted Vietnam to take actions to operate its economy transparently and fairly.

However, after 30 years of economic integration, the country faces a new challenge that is the inertia of many economic management agencies at both central and grassroots levels. After Vietnam became a WTO member, relevant local agencies had yet to issue any guidelines for businesses, except some documents on tariff cuts.

Currently, to implement the new-generation FTAs, Vietnam has to complete a pile of work and change its working methods to be successful. With the new mindset, Vietnam should be well aware of its position in the flow of economic globalization. The country's task is to pave way for that flow.

Vietnam has made anti-corruption progress and the initial results are attributable to the drastic actions taken by high-ranking leaders.

At the same time, it is necessary for the country to draw up a clear integration strategy applicable in the era of economic globalization, focusing on value chain connectivity and development.

A right strategy will create social consensus, and promote joint efforts to pursue a shared goal. Vietnam would lose if it gives no instructions to businesses and localities, and let them look after themselves.

Notetaker: Le Huong

Deciphering "Wars" in a world economic arena

"China must catch up and roll out an economic model different from the freely competitive economic model of the US. If China copies the US economic model, it would always fall behind the US. The competition between the US and China, therefore, is a war between two institutions, which cannot be reconciled"

Nguyen Dinh Luong

Two years after he took office, Donald Trump created chaos in the world economic arena. With his slogans of "America First," and "Make America Great Again," Trump handled a series of international economic commitments of his predecessors by withdrawing from the Trans-Pacific Partnership (TPP), asking for adjustment to or withdrawal from the North American Free Trade Agreement (NAFTA), and withdrawal from the WTO, starting the US-China trade war and imposing sanctions on many countries, including its partners and rivals, etc.

The world is now developing unpredictably with disadvantages.

How will the world economy go on? Will there be any "catastrophe"? To get the answers, we will analyze the world economy first. Today and possibly the next decades, the world economy is operating and developing with three basic components:

-The competition for world domination between powers is getting fiercer, primarily and for the most part in the economic sphere.

-The world economy is operating on the basis of a globalized economy

-The world economy has been operating on the basis of new technical and technological achievements and the 4th Industrial Revolution.

The three factors are parallel and closely linked, producing the foundations, the outcomes and the development momentum to create breakthrough developments for the world economy.

Let's look at the factors.

Competition between powers

The competition between economies is getting fiercer. The strong economic development has led to severe competitions and complexities in the world. All nations want to move ahead and catch up with or even surpass others.

The previous century witnessed the competition between socialism and capitalism. Today, the competition between the US and China is the most extreme one. Any competition, however, must take place in a healthy manner.

To win the competition, China must roll out an economic model different from the freely competitive economic model of the US. If China copies the US economic model, it would always fall behind the US. China has designed an economic model mainly based on big State-owned economic groups, while considering its geostrategic calculations. The country's "One Belt, One Road" strategy has been rolled out mainly through State-owned enterprises. The US economy's strength lies with the power of capitalist groups. Meanwhile, State-owned groups have driven the Chinese economy. The competition between the US and China, therefore, is a competition between two different types of institutions, which cannot be reconciled. A trade war is thus inevitable. If there is a coincidence of this war, it would have been prompted by the mercurial temperament and aggressiveness of Donald Trump, the 45th US President.

Unlike the previous periods, the present competition is taking place amidst economic globalization and the new industrial revolution, making it fiercer.

Economic globalization

To view the issues regarding economic globalization in a less controversial light, we should look at phenomena in the present global economy:

1.The world economy has been a connected one where economies are linked together globally, and value chains are formed and operating across economic realms. Although the Vietnamese economy is standing at a lower level, it has been connected to the regional and global economy. The connectivity cannot be disrupted now and has become more intensive and extensive. The country advocates more intensive and extensive connectivity to grow further.

2. The legal corridor to operate a globalized economy has been institutionalized within the legal framework of WTO as well as the legal frameworks of more than 160 WTO member countries, including Vietnam. Joining the organization, these member economies have to adjust their legal systems to make them match WTO rules.

The WTO rules cover trade liberalization, the implementation of an open economy and fair, transparent economic activities with no discrimination between domestic and foreign firms, etc.

Donald Trump, the 45th President of the US who wants to "Make America Great Again", has rolled out a number of policies like reducing domestic tax and forcing US firms to bring back production from overseas, with some achievements recorded.

The US, under Trump's administration, had not applied WTO rules but used its own rules to impose sanctions on many countries, including its rivals and partners, although it is a WTO member. The situation has stirred up a movement against trade protectionism and a push for freer trade.

The US announced no support for trade protectionism, asking for fairness, saying it wanted to take back what it had lost. The US economy is developing on the foundation of globalization. Without the world market, there will be no US economy. The US economy has been connected to the global economy.

The world, primarily its major powers, is calling for a reform in WTO, which is a must.

The reform does not mean breaking or re-designing the legal framework of the organization.

The reform may refer to dealing with shortcomings formed during the existence of the WTO, restoring the balance of interests, re-designing operational methods to raise the legal efficiency of WTO rules.

WTO came into force as from January 1, 1995 on the basis of the Marrakesh Agreement signed on April 15, 1994 when all of the deals reached through the Uruguay round were considered progressive and acceptable. For example, the car import tax would be over 2 percent, 10 percent or 20 percent in some countries, significantly dropping from the rates of 100 percent or 200 percent imposed earlier.

However, it is not fair to maintain these original commitments after more than two decades, which requires changes and negotiations again.

With more than 160 member countries, the WTO has become a big club that is hard to manage.

3. The legal framework for the globalization has been upgraded and expanded in new-generation FTAs.

The WTO mainly deals with trade issues and those directly relating to trade. Unlike the WTO, new-generation FTAs such as CPTPP, EVFTA and NAFTA or bilateral free trade agreements between the US and Singapore, the Republic of Korea (RoK), Chile, Jordan, Australia and New Zealand, among others, have been upgraded and expanded.

Apart from WTO-like commitments, the agreements adjusted investment ties in accordance with international standards, with intensive and extensive commitments in modern services such as telecoms, finance, internet and e-commerce, among others.

Unlike the WTO, the new-generation FTAs deal with a range of institutional issues such as the management of a national economy, competition policy, State-owned enterprises, public procurement, small and medium-sized enterprises, anti-corruption, labor, environment, and even the recruitment of public servants, etc.

Trump asked for the reform of NAFTA, triggering public concern. The agreement was then amended and the new deal was signed by leaders of the US, Canada and Mexico on December 1, 2018 at a G20 meeting in Argentina.

The negotiations and adjustments of the NAFTA have not broken its legal framework but adjusted and supplemented a number of commitments relating to import tariffs and market opening to better ensure the balance of interest as compared with the pact inked in 1995, while tightening sanctions to raise the efficiency of the agreement. The free trade agreement between the US and the RoK has also been adjusted in that way.

In the past, the competition between economies took place in separate sectors and regions. However, it is now seen across the global economy, notably the competition between the US and China. Disputes occur even in island countries each with a population of only few hundreds of thousands.

Industrial Revolution 4.0

-The 4th Industrial Revolution and new technological achievements have rapidly changed the structure of the global economic structure, production structure, product structure, consumer structure, consumer habits, labor structure, economic management and administration, and daily activities of people.

-Previously, scientific and technological achievements and inventions were put into use gradually, at different paces and in different sectors. Currently, in the globalization environment, they are applied globally to exploit natural and human resources. The 4th Industrial Revolution is accelerating globalization more intensively and extensively.

-Unlike previous periods, scientific and technological application now aims to utilize brain power – an unlimited resource.

-Previously, economies competed for markets and consumers. They are now racing to gain brain power, and the "fight" has got fiercer. Chinese telecoms groups such as ZTE and Huawei have been under pressure in many countries.

Unexpected things about CPTPP through the lens of an international negotiator

"The Vietnam-US Bilateral Trade Agreement (BTA) puts pressure on Vietnam to quit the centrally-planned economy. The CPTPP, however, is expected to drive the country to the modern market economy"

Cao Cuong-Hoang Ly (CafeF.vn – March 8, 2018)

From your perspective, without the US, are there any noteworthy things in the signing of the CPTPP by 11 countries special?

First, the event marked the first-ever formation of a free trade area in Asia-Pacific region, which had been seen in some other regions in the world. Second, the CPTPP offers a new playing field for powers and developed economies like Japan, Australia, Canada and Singapore, among others.

Third, the formation of the CPTPP has created an impulse to further promote globalization and international economic integration. Globalization has not been stopped as presumed by many people.

Finally, it can be said that the 11 member countries' resolve to "rescue" the TPP and reach the final stage without the US has encouraged the country to return. If the 11 countries had not made efforts, the CPTPP could not be formed, let alone the possibility that the US would return.

Why do the 11 CPTPP member countries want to welcome the US back?

The CPTPP member countries want and work to welcome the US back for several reasons. The US accounts for up to 62 percent of total GDP of 12 TPP member countries. The US's participation will give more strength to the block's economy and politics.

The TPP's geopolitical position will be different, and the US will be the main pillar of the TPP, making the TPP more sustainable. As a result, the free trade area will become a magnet and quickly lure the participation of other countries like India, the RoK and Thailand, etc.

The CPTPP has suspended 20 provisions, mostly sought by the US earlier. These provisions have not been removed forever in anticipation of the US return. However, there is no sign of the US return under Trump's administration. The agreement should be restructured to welcome back the US.

Some said China will replace the US in the TPP. What do you think about the possibility?

China remains a big country that follows its own path. The country has acknowledged benefits brought about by globalization and optimized it in its own ways. I think China's strategic choice is not the TPP, but the "One Belt, One Road" (OBOR).

The way China optimizes globalization in its reform is also different from other countries. China uses "steel fists" that are State-owned economic groups pioneering in penetrating foreign markets, followed by the flow of consumer goods in lower segments. It is hard for China to join the TPP as the deal gathers market economies with stringent regulations on state firms, protectionism, subsidies and intellectual property, etc, which are not easy for China to accept.

As you said, the TPP has stringent market principles which China has yet to satisfy. However, the Vietnamese economy itself is somewhat similar to China's, with the operation of state-owned economic groups. Why can Vietnam join the TPP but China cannot?

In the past, state firms in Vietnam always made up the lion's share of the national economy and dominated the operation of others. However, private enterprises are now on the rise, and are considered the momentum for economic growth. The Government has taken drastic measures to reform mechanisms and policies, towards a "growth-enabling" Government, and cut unnecessary business conditions, while speeding up the equitization of state enterprises, which have been seen as positive changes for the adaptation.

How do you evaluate economic benefits through the statistics regarding GDP and exports Vietnam has recorded since joining the CPTPP?

In this regard, the media mainly focuses on growth rate and export-import expansion when mentioning economic benefits brought about by the CPTPP to Vietnam. However, such economic benefits, in my opinion, are not really yet visible, like "counting chickens before they hatch."

I think that Vietnam has, for the first time, begun to join a playing field for open, developed market economies. As compared with FTAs Vietnam has signed, the CPTPP is a new type, a new "rule of game", and a new level of globalization.

Initially, I think that this would create major changes and transformation in economic management and administration in Vietnam if the country seriously observes the commitments. Each word and sentence in the 8,000-page deal has its own meaning, referring to rights and obligations. They are not written "for fun."

The CPTPP offers a legal framework to operate a modern economy, a detailed set of rules to regulate and lead the Vietnamese economy to a fair playing field with developed countries, a roadmap to set rules for an open economy with high international criteria, and a pure and health economic environment. The pact includes commitments regarding rights and obligations towards building a large-scale free trade area. It is also a roadmap for Vietnam to raise its economic capacity.

While the US-Vietnam Bilateral Trade Agreement prompted Vietnam to quit its centrally-planned economy, the CPTPP requires the country to embark on a modern market economy. The CPTPP, for example, stipulates corruption-related issues, from the concept of corruption to groups that often take bribes and commit corruption, and policy loopholes causing corruption.

I believe that if Vietnam seriously follows the provisions, it will see corruption reducing. Vietnam will integrate more intensively and effectively in the world if the country can successfully build a developed market economy.

The TPP remains attractive without the US

"The US was once the main economic pillar of the TPP. Without the pillar, its frame would be weaker and deformed in the face of storms. Without the US, the TPP has lost a source of momentum and strong pressure for the implementation"

Vo Van Thanh (VnExpress-2017)

The former BTA Chief Negotiator is optimistic about the TPP's future without the US.

TPP member countries are scheduled to meet on the sidelines of the APEC Economic Leaders' Meeting in early November in Vietnam's Da Nang city to make final decisions.

Nguyen Dinh Luong, former BTA Chief Negotiator, granted an interview to VnExpress, during which he shared his views as a negotiation expert.

-What do you hope for the upcoming meeting of the TPP member countries?

-The TPP was signed on February 4, 2016 in Auckland, New Zealand by 12 member countries after five years of negotiations. However, President Donald Trump signed an executive order on January 23, just a few days after taking office, withdrawing the US from the agreement. The remaining 11 member countries have recently met and held several rounds of talks. Although official information has yet to be released, I hope and believe that the countries will reach consensus during the 2017 APEC Economic Leaders'

Meeting to continue the TPP without the US. All of the countries, primarily stronger economies like Japan, Australia and New Zealand, have seen benefits to be brought about by the deal.

So, there will be a TPP without the US, while it was considered a "product" mainly promoted by Americans. How do you evaluate this?

-The US held the "trump card" in TPP negotiations. What was achieved in the TPP aimed to ensure interests of the US and its economic groups first. It is also a product of globalization. Once globalization is promoted, the world economy will more be open, thus benefiting the US and its economic groups more.

Without the US, the TPP has experienced certain disappointments. First, the US was once the main economic pillar of the TPP. Without the pillar, its frame would be weaker and deformed in the face of storms. The US accounts for 62 percent of the regional GDP and with a big market, it serves as a destination for other countries worldwide. The TPP member countries hoped for the US market when they decided to join the agreement.

Second, without the US, the TPP has lost a source of momentum and pressure to push ahead with the implementation. The US's "authority" lies with not only its strength in the economic arena, but also its collected strength in other fields.

For Vietnam, as far as I can see since the BTA became effective in 2001, the country often considers economic and trade commitments with the US more seriously.

-Without the US, the remaining 11 TPP member countries will have to review the agreement's content, making it match the new situation. In your opinion, how will the agreement be adjusted?

-Representatives from the 11 countries have met recently to discuss this matter. I believe that there will be only a handful of adjustments to the TPP, which are also not important, because the remaining member countries hope for the US return. To welcome the US back, they should not remove what was set up by the country, especially in labor, environment, intellectual property, public procurement, transparency, anti-corruption, dispute settlement, competition policy, and other services of the US's strength.

The possibility of the US return to the TPP should not be ruled out soon. President Trump wanted to roll back Obama's legacy, but the past nearly one year has proven that it is not easy.

More importantly, the TPP serves the interests of many US groups that will not easily see their interests cut. They will unite, act and seek ways to preserve the interests.

-The remaining 11 TPP member countries would reach final decisions in Da Nang. What should Vietnam do to optimize the agreement?

-Vietnam has maintained its clear and sound view backing the continuity of the TPP. What to do and how to do to optimize the deal require in-depth discussions. I just want to mention it briefly.

The TPP and the EU-Vietnam Free Trade Agreement (EVFTA) (known as new-generation FTAs) fully prescribes rules, regulations and sanctions that help Vietnam build a better business environment, catch up with the flow of globalization and bring it into full play.

Over the past three decades, Vietnam was still like a bobbing boat in the flow of globalization. Although the country has made progress and reaped certain achievements, there is a lack of a well-designed integration strategy.

Vietnam has adjusted and supplemented its legal system, mainly due to pressure from international commitments, but not the country's proactiveness. It has worked to re-design the market economy, also mainly due to competition pressure.

Therefore, with the new mindset, we need to be well aware of Vietnam's position in the flow of globalization, and look at unmatched points between the Vietnamese market economy and the world market economy.

With such factors, I believe that the TPP will remain attractive without the US and generally the new-generation FTAs will continue to give a boost to the market and investment. Notably, with regulations and commitments in the agreements, Vietnam must move forward to operate an open, transparent, fair economy. This is a new development step.

-What should Vietnam do first in anticipation of the TPP?

Regulations in the TPP and EVFTA have not allowed barriers to integration flow, and would help Vietnam deal with problems.

Once both the TPP and EVFTA take effect, there must be programs and plans to seriously materialize commitments. It is worthy of note that the agreements only come into force when preparations (such as adjustments and amendments to laws) are satisfactory.

It is a must to draw up a scientific integration strategy, focusing on value-chain connecting and building. The strategy must take into account the economic benefits of Vietnam, as well as requirements and development trends of the world economy, and must be connected with the 4th Industrial Revolution.

A correct strategy will create social consensus in implementation and pursuing common goals, with no one left behind and no space for negative factors of the market economy.

Benefit pie is hardly divided equally

(Presentation at the Workshop on the National Assembly with negotiations, ratification and implementation of free trade agreements - April 2014).

"There is no way that the benefit pie will be divided equally among all participants of the globalization fest. Those who are stronger and excel will get more. Vietnam must have a competitive market economy to reap the benefits"

Nguyen Dinh Luong

"The impact of new-generation FTAs on Vietnam: opportunities and challenges" has emerged as a major issue. There should be a national scientific research study with the participation of Vietnamese scientists to look into it and make necessary conclusions.

The four speakers at the workshop will share their own views on this issue.

Let me present some preliminary ideas.

Ladies and gentlemen

Economic globalization is quickly developing and connecting almost all economies in the world by "magic wands" of trans-national corporations.

Since its inception in January 1, 1995, the WTO has basically removed protection barriers, creating an open playing field for the world economy. However, it has become a club with diverse and complex members that have failed to reach consensus in designing a new legal framework more intensive and extensive for the globalized economy. The Doha round has made no progress and got stuck.

Given this, countries have no choice but to break the barriers to find a more open, free playground, leading to the formation of FTAs, both bilateral and regional.

Where do FTAs receive support?

Africans have yet to engage in FTAs as they are still busy earning their living. Those who speak the Arabic language also have no time to talk about FTAs as they are still stuck in the "Arab Spring." The FTAs are mainly discussed by the rich and those who want to get rich quickly, especially in North America, Europe and Asia.

How many types of FTAs are there?

FTAs have different forms, levels and scopes of commitments, depending on development and strategic intentions of participating countries. There are:

-FTAs with lower commitments and narrower scopes like those between ASEAN and such partners as China, India, Japan and the Republic of Korea. The FTAs mainly focus on export-import tariff cuts and market opening to facilitate the free circulation of goods, and other fields like investment, services and intellectual property, etc. Their commitment scopes remain limited or generally less binding.

- FTAs with more sustainable, higher, tighter commitments between the US and Canada, Australia, Singapore, China and the Republic of Korea. They cover trade, services, investment, intellectual property, public procurement, commitments by State-owned enterprises, environment and labor. They can be considered new-generation FTAs.

- Once the negotiations are completed, the TPP would be the newest, most advanced FTA with the most intensive, extensive commitments and the strictest regulations.

The TPP is called a "new-generation agreement", a "21st century agreement", a club of economic freedom supporters and a playground for the rich.

Vietnamese Party and State leaders bravely decided to join the high-class playing field. Vietnamese people's dream of "standing on an equal footing with world powers across the five continents" might come true if Vietnam succeeds in the game.

Matter: Impact of new-generation FTAs on Vietnam: opportunities and challenges

At this point, Vietnam has not joined any new-generation FTAs yet. The US has yet to negotiate a bilateral FTA with Vietnam. Meanwhile, the Southeast Asian nation is in TPP talks. Joining the TPP also means engaging in a new-generation FTA. Therefore, please let me analyze the TPP's impact on Vietnam.

With its content and participant structure, the TPP has geopolitical importance, with both temporary impact on trade growth and long-term, profound impact on Vietnam's institutions, development path, guidelines and policies. The following impacts are long-term and would generate both opportunities and challenges, depending on Vietnam's capacity to handle them.

* First impact

The TPP will create moral and legal pressure, prompting Vietnam to build a competitive market economy.

The TPP playing field is set for market economies with high and very high competitiveness, as well as open and very open economies, particularly the US, Japan, Canada, Australia and Singapore that always top the global competitiveness index.

The TPP game takes place on the basis of globalization for which these countries have made the best preparations and kept ready to exploit its advantages. There is no way that the benefit pie will be shared equally among all participants of the globalization fest. Those who are stronger and excel will get more. Vietnam must have a competitive market economy to reap the benefits. "If you are not excellent and strong, you would always be a caddie."

Vietnam should not hold the penultimate position in the global value chain forever, and should quit the road of labor-intensive growth.

The very stringent regulations of the TPP show the need to abolish all not belonging to the market economy, which would impact institutions, economic administration and social management. And Vietnam has made profound changes in its economic administration.

After fulfilling commitments in the TPP, Vietnam will properly have a market economy, and won't need to appeal to countries to recognize its market economy.

***Second impact**

The TPP will create both conditions and pressure for Vietnam to develop a strong contingent of businesses.

To win in a war, a good staff is not enough. There must be talented commanders and well-trained soldiers. Similarly, outstanding enterprises make successes in the trade sector. Economic globalization has been seen as a race between tycoons and trans-national groups that have advantages in capital, technology, production and marketing. They dominate the world consumer taste as well as national and international policies. They are now present everywhere. The trans-national groups are implementing the biggest and most important projects in Vietnam.

The State only fulfills the growth-enabling role and creates a suitable legal framework as well as optimal conditions for people and businesses to operate. The business community represents the nation and the strength of the national economy. A strong economy should not accommodate weak businesses, as proven in the US, Japan, the Republic of Korea or any other economies.

Vietnam must build up a new, strong contingent of enterprises to gain successes in the globalization race. The businesses, of course, should not be Vinashin, Vinaline and "billionaires" emerging from land flips. Such "billionaires" are unable to compete in the world market where there are no land price differences thanks to not having an unclear law like in Vietnam. On the contrary, such firms as Viettel and FPT should be nurtured to grow further, and there must be tens of thousands of stronger enterprises.

The stringent rules define rights and obligations of foreign investors, and the need to facilitate their operation in a free economy and absolutely ensure their interests.

Vietnam must have talents to work together with foreigners to exploit domestic and foreign markets, including TPP member countries, like they are doing in Vietnam. Big, competitive businesses can take on the task.

***Third impact**

The TPP creates opportunities and moral and legal pressure on Vietnam to consolidate a rule-of-law State.

There are some must-do tasks:

The first task is to perfect and modernize the legal system

Most TPP member countries have the complete and modern legal system of a developed nation.

With a complete and modern legal system, Vietnam would protect its interests. Meanwhile, an incomplete legal system would push the country into disadvantages and losses.

The US boasts the most comprehensive and advanced legal system that also serves as a legal corridor to operate the globalized economy. The legal system is strong enough to protect the interests of the US and Americans anywhere, and protect US firms anywhere. The country has worked hard to gradually internationalize its legal system through the WTO as well as FTA and TPP.

Vietnamese legislators for their 2001-2005 tenure grappled with the reform and amendment of the domestic legal system, from a monopolistic, centrally-planned economy to a market economy, with no discrimination as committed in the US-Vietnam BTA, and in preparation for joining the WTO. They might get another headache in integrating new concepts and standards the US imposed in the TPP, into the domestic legal system. This would be an opportunity for Vietnam to modernize its legal system to adapt to economic globalization.

The second task is to consolidate judicial assistance organizations that support businesses in integration.

-Building up a strong legal system

-Building up a strong arbitration system

-Building up a network of strong legal assistance agencies (bar association, notary, assessment).

-Building up a good information system

-Training good legal experts, completing the network of good legal consultation organizations (Vietnam has to hire foreign consultants in international lawsuits).

Without a strong legal system, Vietnamese firms cannot maintain their foothold in the global game, even in the domestic market.

The third task is to build up culture of "living and working in accordance with law."

-People should understand and respect the law, and avoid violations.

-Businesses should operate in accordance with the law, avoid violations and have no intentions of taking advantages of loopholes in law, and tax evasion for profits.

-Public servants must grasp laws to guide the implementation, and conduct regular inspections and supervisions. Concerned officials need to make field trips to handle emerging issues.

- Living and working in accordance with laws has become a popular culture, and there is no reason for Vietnam to do otherwise.

More effort needed after joining the WTO

"Vietnam has to grow stronger when joining the WTO. To that end, the country and its businesses have to improve themselves and "integrate" first, and should not stop at the "WTO membership"

Dinh Chuc (Labour, December 16, 2005)

Nguyen Dinh Luong may be the oldest among the Vietnamese negotiators in an economic agreement with the US.

One winter afternoon five years ago (after the signing of the US-Vietnam BTA), I had a chance to listen to his story about the five years of negotiations.

It was a really long journey as during the five years, Luong travelled between Vietnam and US for nearly 20 times, and patiently joined tens of talks of different scales. His efforts paid off as the BTA was finally reached on July 13, 2000.

Although he has retired, Luong kept close eyes on the WTO Ministerial Conference in Hong Kong this afternoon, and felt worried: If the Doha round ends soon, Vietnam will face more difficulties.

Our conversation focused on a new topic: Vietnam's path towards the WTO next year.

It is a must to understand Americans and America well

Luong said his biggest experience in the negotiations is understanding deeply, thoroughly and comprehensively partners. To understand them, there is no way but to optimize meetings of all levels, even the break time.

You should not dominate the talks. In a one-hour meeting, for example, you should give your partners 50 minutes to present their ideas, and spend only 10 minutes answering their questions. You should enable your partners to expose their intentions.

How did you approach the US in the BTA negotiations?

My first task was learning about America and Americans. I searched libraries, met experts in US studies, and carefully studied the US's legal system, economy, culture and social affairs.

I also analyzed China's WTO negotiations with the US as Vietnam and China share similarities. I tried to figure out why the neighboring country could not enter WTO (predecessor the General Agreement on Tariffs and Trade – GATT) after 14-15 years of talks.

How did you understand the US?

The US is totally different from any other partners. I still remember what former US Trade Representative Barshefsky said: The US always targets package agreements in economic negotiations.

In negotiations, the US often uses the "bulldozer" strategy. They solve problems as a whole package, not separately like other partners. In duty talks, for example, they scan from the first tax line to the 10,000th, not separately like the EU has done for wine and medicines, and Japan for auto.

Is it clear that the US sets higher requirements than other partners?

A decision to admit a new member is taken, in principle, by a two-thirds majority vote. In fact, it is a problem if the US has yet to greenlight. The US's unwritten role in WTO has been accepted. This explained why many countries had not actively negotiated with Vietnam, and just waited until the end of Vietnam-US talks to give a nod.

Do personal relations play any role in negotiations?

Yes, but in other aspects. I was determined to establish long-term relations and build up trust through negotiations. I prefer honesty and frankness which Americans like most. They trusted and offered me "tips" on what can be accepted and what needs no more bargaining. This is the advantage of "personal relations."

Qualitative of "gains and "losses"

I learnt about the meeting between Truong Dinh Tuyen, Vietnamese Trade Minister, and Pascal Lamy, former EU Commissioner for Trade (present WTO General Director). Tuyen frankly asked Lamy whether it was unfair when developed countries set too high requirements for their poor partners. Lamy admitted this, further saying "Such is life." Tuyen then asked the US side to reduce the unfairness, saying Vietnam will accept the "Such is life" and move ahead. "Once we reach consensus on the path, Vietnam will join WTO," Tuyen said.

Luong said the "moving ahead" and "reducing unfairness" are the acceptability of "gains" and "losses." However, what is worth losing, let it go soon. What can be gained, try to get it.

Luong said: "We are protecting some economic sectors where we have no competitive edge. The protection just provides Vietnamese consumers and State with products whose quality is lower than international standards and price is much higher than that in the international market."

You just mentioned a number of sectors. Do "sensitive areas" and key economic sectors need protection in countries?

Actually, "gains" and "losses" here just refer to qualitative, not quantitative. Such "Gains" and "losses" can be made during the long process of joining WTO and must be assessed from the "dynamic" not "static" perspective.

However, it must be clear that there are things we cannot lose and we must resolutely protect them. What is worth losing (often domestic losses) such as the monopoly of some industries and State subsidy should be abolished.

Some said many domestic firms are not strong enough and they need to be incubated more. What do you think about this?

I strongly oppose the idea of closing the door to help domestic firms grow stronger. They must have chances to compete and gain experience.

So, integration is an inevitable trend, not a selection, isn't it?

That's right. It is a mistake to consider integration a must as globalization is an irreversible trend and we have no other choice but to accept it.

I need honest criticism

Luong said the media reported many negotiators or foreign officials coming to Vietnam, giving both praise and criticism to the country. Everyone likes praise, but Luong wants and seriously looks into their constructive criticism.

Among the guests to Vietnam, he was interested in opinions of Pascal Lamy (present WTO General Secretary), Barshefsky (former US Trade Representative) and Mike Moore (former WTO General Secretary).

They shared the view that Vietnam has to stay stronger when joining WTO. Vietnam and its firms have to improve themselves and "integrate" first, and should not stop at the WTO membership. He further said: "I like frankness. Guests often give more applause than criticism. Compliments are often made for diplomatic purposes, so we should not consider them as their official assessment. If we know how to analyze their criticism and suggestions, we will join WTO sooner."

Did you set any targets for negotiations?

Of course, each period of negotiations has its own targets. During the final round, negotiators often foresee the outcomes, and they will work towards them.

Where is Vietnam standing in the roadmap of WTO negotiations with the US?

Vietnam is at the final stage of the negotiations with the US. Therefore, negotiators must foresee the results to accelerate the process.

Our conversation was interrupted when the TV channel aired a group of protesters holding up slogans "Act for the poor" outside the WTO conference. Looking at the statue featuring "the rich living on the backs of the poor" placed on a street in Hong Kong when the protest passed through, Luong sighed: More effort needed after joining WTO.

"Trade headwinds" of US President Donald Trump and Chinese President Xi Jinping

"Each country, especially the powers, has its own ways to optimize globalization. They will complete their globalization goal in their own way"

Nguyen Dinh Luong (CafeF.vn - 2017)

US President Donald Trump promotes bilateral trade and criticizes multilateral relations causing inequality. Meanwhile, Chinese President Xi Jinping affirmed: "Globalization is an irreversible trend."

The Ariyana international convention centre has recently drawn the attention of the international community with the presence of leaders from the world's two leading economies.

From the airport, President Donald Trump went straight to the centre to begin his speech. After applauding member economies for their achievements, he candidly said the core of the partnership lies with fairness and reciprocity.

The President said although the US reduced trade barriers, and allowed foreign goods to flow freely into the US, other countries didn't open their markets to the US. He also condemned the countries that have not observed principles on intellectual property and market access, among others. He held that the US has been treated unequally and got no benefits from games, which hurt the US and its people.

Trump also stated that the trade deficit the US ran with the China was "unacceptable." Although he did not criticize Beijing, he said this is an opportunity to look back and correct mistakes.

Trump said from this day forward, the US will compete on a fair and equal basis, and not to be taken advantage of anymore, with the motto of "America First." The US was ready to cooperate with countries for mutual benefits. Trump emphasized the signing of bilateral free trade agreements with partners, but noted that "What we will no longer do is enter into large agreements that tie our hands, surrender our sovereignty, and make meaningful enforcement practically impossible."

Xi then presented a different view that supports globalization, which, he said, has contributed to growth over the past decades.

"Globalization is an irreversible trend but the world must work to make it more balanced and inclusive," he said.

"We should uphold multilateralism."

He suggested countries work together to promote investment and development, and create more open and inclusive liberalization, thus bringing benefits to all people.

Calling for support towards the multilateral trading regime and free trade in Asia-Pacific, Xi said the building of a free trade area of the Asia-Pacific (FTAAP) is a long-cherished dream.

The opposite views are interesting as each leader exploited globalization in their own way.

Trumps's view in favor of bilateralism and against multilateralism is not feasible since globalization is inevitable. Whatever Trump does, the US economy is still connected intensively and extensively with the world.

The present economy is the flow that runs to every corner of the world. How can Trump stop it? Stopping the flow is very hard, and his measures would not work.

Besides, whether major US groups will maintain their support of Trump's views in the long run is also an issue. If multilateralism benefits them more, these businesses will certainly not stand still and see opportunities go out of reach.

Therefore, I think that Trump's view in the short term will cause difficulties for multilateral trade, but implementation or changes in the future still should be taken into account.

Meanwhile, Xi's opinions in favor of globalization matched the trend. However, each country, especially powers, optimize globalization in their own way. The US and China have their own way too. They will realize their globalization goals in their own way.

******

Abbreviations in this book

BTA: Bilateral Trade Agreement

FTA*:* Free Trade Agreement

WTO: World Trade Organization

GATT: General Agreement on Tariffs and Trade

TRIMS: Agreement on Trade-related Investment Measures

TPP: Trans-Pacific Partnership

CPTPP: Comprehensive and Progressive Agreement for Trans-Pacific Partnership

EVFTA: European Union-Vietnam Free Trade Agreement

NT: National Treatment

GSP: Generalized System of Preferences

MFN: Most Favoured Nation

NTR: Normal Trade Relations

PNTR: Permanent Normal Trade Relations

USTR: Office of United States Trade Representative

USAID: United States Agency for International Development

ASEAN: Association of South – East Asian Nations

APEC: Asia Pacific Economic Cooperation

ASEM: Asia – Europe Meeting

NAFTA: North American Free Trade Agreement

AFTA: ASEAN Free Trade Area

Marrakesh Agreement: manifested by the Marrakesh Declaration, was an agreement signed in Marrakesh, Morocco, by 123 nations on 15 April 1994, marking the culmination of the 8-year-long Uruguay Round and establishing the World Trade Organization

COMECON: (or SEV; CMEA): The Council for Mutual Economic Assistance

EU: European Union

NATO: North Atlantic Treaty Organization

Key figures in the BTA process

Joseph (Joe) Damond: Chief Negotiator of the US Negotiating delegation for BTA

Mrs Charlene Barshefky: United States Trade Representative, the US top trade negotiator nominated by former President Bill Clinton.

Richard Fisher: Deputy U.S. Trade Representative

Mrs Virginia "Ginny" Foote: a Board member and Chair of AmCham in Vietnam.

Pete Perterson: The first United States Ambassador to Vietnam from 1997 – 2001, after the normalization of the two countries.

Vu Khoan: Vietnamese Minister of Trade during 2000-2002 term

Truong Dinh Tuyen: Vietnamese Minister of Trade during 1997-2000 and 2002-2007

Nguyen Dinh Luong: Chief Negotiator of Vietnam Negotiating delegation on Vietnam-US BTA.

Le Van Bang: Vietnamese Ambassador to the United Stated during 1997-2001

Negotiation rounds of Vietnam US Bilateral Trade Agreement

Round	Date	Location
1	21/9/-29/9/1996	Hà Nội
2	9/2-11/12/1996	Hà Nội
3	12/4-17/4/1997	Hà Nội
4	6/10-11/10/1997	Washington
5	16/5-25/5/1998	Washington
6	12/9-22/9/1998	Hà Nội
7	15/3-19/3/1999	Hà Nội
8	14/6-18/6/1999	Washington
9	23/7-25/7/1999	Hà Nội (at Minister level)
10	28/8-2/9/1999	Washington
11	3/7-13/7/2000	Washington (at Minister level